GOD'S
JUSTICE

D1528192

THE STORY BIBLE SERIES

1. *God's Family* tells the story of creation, God's promises to Abraham's family, and the adventures of Joseph.

2. *God Rescues His People* tells about Israel's escape from Egypt, Moses and the Ten Commandments, and the wandering in the wilderness.

3. *God Gives the Land* tells the story of Joshua, the adventures of the judges, and the story of Ruth.

4. *God's Chosen King* tells about Samuel, Saul, and David, God's promises to David's family, and the Psalms.

5. *God's Wisdom and Power* tells about the glorious reign of Solomon, the wonderful works of Elijah and Elisha, and the Proverbs and the Song of Songs.

6. *God's Justice* tells stories about the prophets who spoke about God's justice, and the fall of Israel and Judah.

   Additional books in the series will tell stories from the Apocrypha and the New Testament.

Story Bible Series, Book 6

GOD'S JUSTICE

Stories from 2 Kings, 2 Chronicles, Amos, Hosea, Isaiah, Micah, Zephaniah, Jeremiah, Nahum, and Habakkuk

Retold by Eve B. MacMaster

Illustrated by James Converse

HERALD PRESS
Scottdale, Pennsylvania
Kitchener, Ontario
1984

Library of Congress Cataloging in Publication Data

MacMaster, Eve, 1942-
  God's justice.

  (Story Bible series; bk. 6)
  Summary: Retells Bible stories in which the Prophets
speak about God's justice and in which the predicted
falls of Israel and Judah come true.
  1. Justice—Biblical teaching—Juvenile literature.
2. Bible stories, English—O.T. Prophets. [1. Bible
stories—O.T. Prophets. 2. Justice—Biblical teaching]
I. Converse, James, ill. II. Title.
BS1199.J8M32 1984   224'.09505   84-20514
ISBN 0-8361-3381-1 (pbk.)

GOD'S JUSTICE
Copyright © 1984 by Herald Press, Scottdale, PA 15683
    Published simultaneously in Canada by Herald Press,
    Kitchener, Ont. N2G 4M5. All rights reserved.
Library of Congress Catalog Card Number: 84-20514
International Standard Book Number: 0-8361-3381-1
Printed in the United States of America
Design: Alice B. Shetler

90 89 88 87 86 85 84 10 9 8 7 6 5 4 3 2 1

The Story of This Book

Several years ago I was looking for a Bible story book to read to my children. I wanted one that was complete, without tacked-on morals or a denominational interpretation. I wanted one that was faithful to the Bible and fun to read. I couldn't find what I was looking for.

With the encouragement of my husband, Richard Mac-Master, I approached Herald Press with the idea of the series: a retelling of the whole Bible with nothing added and nothing subtracted, just following the story line through the Old and New Testaments.

The people at Herald Press were agreeable and enthusiastic and gave much valuable advice, especially book editor Paul M. Schrock.

At his suggestion, I asked some academic and professional people in our community to check the stories for style and accuracy. Members of the advisory committee, who have kindly volunteered their time, include Bible professors George R. Brunk III, Ronald D. Guengerich, G. Irvin Lehman, and Kenneth Seitz; childhood curriculum and librarian specialists Elsie G. Lehman and A. Arlene Bumbaugh; and book marketing specialist Angie B. Williams.

I hope this series will lead its readers to the original, for no retelling is a substitute for the Bible itself. The Bible is actually a collection of books written over a long period of time in a variety of forms. It has been translated and retold in every generation, because people everywhere want to know what God is like.

The main character in every story is God. The plot of every story is God's activity among his people: creating, saving, fighting, reigning, and doing works of wisdom and power.

The first book in the series is *God's Family*. It tells stories about God the Creator.

The second book is *God Rescues His People*. It tells stories about God the Savior.

The third book is *God Gives the Land*. It tells stories about God the warrior.

The fourth book, *God's Chosen King*, tells stories about God the true King.

The fifth book, *God's Wisdom and Power*, tells stories about God, the source of wisdom and power.

This book, *God's Justice*, tells stories about God the righteous Judge.

This volume is dedicated to the people of God today who are working for peace and justice.

—Eve MacMaster
Bridgewater, Virginia
Independence Day, 1984

Contents

The Fall of Samaria

The Lion Roars

2 Kings 14; Amos 1—2, 4—6

IN the silence of the wilderness of Judah, Amos the shepherd was watching over his sheep. He stood on the rocky hillside and looked out at his flock. The animals were grazing quietly.

Suddenly he heard a wild, strange sound. His muscles tensed as he looked around the hillside for signs of danger.

The sound continued. His whole body listened. What was it? It sounded like a mighty voice thundering across the land, like a roll of thunder before the breaking of a great storm. No ... it was more

like the roar of a pouncing, attacking lion. . . .

It was the voice of God. Amos trembled with fear as the Lord God spoke to him. He heard things no human being had ever heard. He saw visions no human being had ever seen.

Then the voice was gone and Amos was alone again with the animals. He was still frightened, but he obeyed the words of the Lord. He found someone else to look after his sheep, and then he headed north, to the kingdom of Israel.

These were the days when Jeroboam II was king, and Amos found great wealth in Israel. No enemy had threatened the borders of the kingdom since Jeroboam had defeated the Arameans, so the Israelites were concentrating their energy on becoming rich.

Amos saw the magnificent mansions that the wealthy landowners, officials, and merchants of Israel had built with their new riches. Some of these people were so successful, they owned two houses—one for summer and one for winter.

Amos reached the city of Bethel on a feast day. Men, women, and children from the capital city of Samaria and all the other towns and villages of Israel were coming to worship at the great national temple.

Priests in fine robes were taking offerings while other priests were burning sacrifices on the altar. The smell of roasted meat hung in the air above the crowd as smoke from the altar rose into the clear sky and drifted across the rocky hills.

The temple musicians played harps, lyres, and cymbals. The people sang hymns and prayed aloud to the Lord. That day at Bethel the Israelites were so busy with their sacrifices, music, and prayers, they didn't notice the stranger in the crowd.

Suddenly Amos stepped out and cried, "Hear the word of the Lord!"

The people stopped and stared at the stranger.

"Listen!" he cried. "The Lord is going to punish the nations. He'll judge them for all their crimes. They've committed such terrible sins, he's going to destroy their cities. He'll strike them all: the Arameans, the Philistines, the Phoenicians, the Edomites, the Ammonites, and the Moabites."

The people listened eagerly to Amos as he described the crimes of the nations and the disasters the Lord was going to send to them. How pleasant it was to hear about their neighbors' sins!

But then Amos said, "The Lord is going to punish Israel. He's angry because the rich people have been cheating the poor! They lie and steal and bribe judges! Merchants use false weights and overcharge their customers. They sell poor folks into slavery when they can't pay their debts.

"The rich men and women of Samaria anoint themselves with fine oil and lie on ivory couches listening to music and drinking wine by the bowlful. They stuff their mansions with luxuries, but they don't care a bit about the suffering of the poor.

"The Lord will judge Israel for breaking his commandments and ignoring his teachings. He's going to send an enemy nation to invade the land and take away your riches.

"The wealthy men will be the first to be taken prisoner. And the rich women of Samaria—those fat cows—they'll suffer for their greed. The mansions of Samaria will completely disappear."

The worshipers at Bethel didn't like Amos's message. They didn't believe a word he said. How could God punish them? They were the chosen people. God had blessed them with wealth and power. He would never treat them like other nations—never!

"Yes," said Amos. "The Lord did choose Israel from all the nations of the earth. But he chose you because he loved you, not because you're better than other people. He rescued you from slavery in Egypt and brought you into this land. He gave you everything you need. He taught you how to live, but you have disobeyed him."

The Israelites were shocked. What about their beautiful worship services—their offerings, their music, their prayers?

"Your worship means nothing to God!" cried Amos. "You pray to him while you cheat your neighbors.

"Hear what the Lord says to you:

I hate and despise your feasts;
  I loathe your religious ceremonies!

I reject your offerings;
  I refuse your sacrifices!

Stop your noisy singing;
  I won't listen to your music!

But let justice roll down like a river,
  and righteousness like an ever-flowing stream!

"For many years the Lord has sent prophets to warn you, but you told them not to speak. When he sent small disasters to get your attention, you kept on ignoring him.

"So now the Lord is preparing to send a great disaster. This time you'll pay attention.

"The day of the Lord is coming, and it will be a day of judgment. Israel, prepare to meet your God!"

2

Ripe Fruit

Amos 3, 7—9

When God spoke to Amos, he showed him visions of the future. First Amos saw a swarm of grasshoppers, ready to eat all the plants growing in the fields.

"Lord God!" he cried. "Have mercy, I beg you. Don't let these grasshoppers destroy the crops. The people will starve. Israel is so small and weak—how can they stand it?"

"I won't let it happen," answered the Lord.

Then Amos saw the Lord himself sending fire to destroy the land.

"Stop, Lord God, I beg you!" he cried. "How can Israel stand it, being so small and weak?"

"This won't happen either," answered the Lord.

The Lord sent Amos three more visions to show what was going to happen if the people of Israel didn't change their way of living. Each vision was more terrible than the last, for the Lord was becoming angrier and angrier.

In the third vision Amos saw the Lord standing beside a wall, holding a long cord with a weight on the end of it. He was using this plumb line to test the wall, to measure how straight it was.

"What do you see, Amos?" asked the Lord.

"A plumb line," he answered.

"Look, Amos. I'm going to test my people to see whether they're crooked or straight. I won't overlook their crimes anymore. I'll punish King Jeroboam's family. They'll die by the sword. They'll suffer violent death as punishment for their wickedness."

Then Amos saw another vision.

"What do you see?" asked the Lord.

"A basket of ripe fruit," he answered.

"Israel is like the fruit," said the Lord. "They're ripe for destruction. I won't show mercy to them anymore, for they're cruel to the poor. They cheat in business, and they steal from the needy. I'm going to send a great disaster to the land!"

In the fifth vision Amos saw the Lord standing beside the altar.

"Strike the pillars!" shouted the Lord. "Let the

roof fall down on their heads. Don't let anyone escape."

Amos told the people at Bethel about his visions. He explained that the Lord's anger was increasing because their sins were increasing. The Lord had tested them and found that they were crooked. They were ripe for destruction. Soon he would let the roof fall down on their heads.

Day after day Amos spoke at Bethel, and every day Amaziah the high priest listened to him carefully. Finally, Amaziah became so angry, he sent a report to the king.

"Amos is plotting against you among the people," he said. "The land can't stand any more of his preaching. He's been saying terrible things about Israel. And now he's telling the people you'll die by the sword, Israel will be defeated, and the people will be carried away into exile."

Then Amaziah returned to the temple. "Go away, prophet!" he cried. "Go back home to Judah, and earn your living there. We don't want any more of your talk here. Bethel is the royal sanctuary, the national temple of Israel."

"I'm not a professional prophet," answered Amos. "I don't belong to a community of prophets. I'm a shepherd and a tree farmer. I'm here only because the Lord sent me. He took me from my sheep and told me to prophesy to his people.

When the lion roars,
who isn't afraid?

When the Lord God speaks,
who can refuse to prophesy?

"Now listen to the word of the Lord. You say, 'Don't prophesy against Israel.' Therefore, the Lord says, 'You and your family will be destroyed. Your land will be taken away from you, and you'll die in a foreign country. And the people of Israel will be taken into captivity.' "

Amos's messages were frightening, but before he left Bethel, he gave the people of Israel some messages of hope, too.

"If you turn to the Lord," said Amos, "he'll save you. If you seek good, and not evil, if you do justice to your neighbors, then the Lord will really be with you, as you say he is now. He'll take pity on you and rescue you from your enemies.

"Although the Lord has decided to punish you, he won't destroy you completely. He'll leave a small band of survivors, a remnant of Israel. And someday he'll bring that remnant back and bless them. And they'll live forever in the land the Lord their God has given to them."

The Unfaithful Wife and Her Loving Husband

2 Kings 15; Hosea

A few years after the Lord called Amos to be a prophet, he called another man, Hosea, to bring his word to the people.

The first time the Lord spoke to Hosea, he told him to get married, and Hosea married a woman named Gomer.

When their first child was born, the Lord spoke to Hosea again. "Name the boy Jezreel," he said, "for soon I'll punish Jeroboam's family. I'll put an end to their rule and break the power of Israel."

The boy's name was a sign that the Lord was going to judge the royal family, as Amos had prophesied. Jezreel was the place where Jeroboam's great grandfather, Jehu, had massacred the family of Ahab and made himself king. Now Jehu's family had become as wicked as the kings they had replaced.

Soon after the birth of Hosea's son Jezreel, King Jeroboam II of Israel died, and his son Zechariah became king. Six months later a man named Shallum assassinated Zechariah and set himself up as king. Just a month later, a man named Menahem assassinated Shallum.

Menahem ruled for ten years. He was a cruel king, who massacred an entire city. Next came Menahem's son Pekahiah, who reigned for two years. Then an army officer named Pekah assassinated him and became king. God's word was coming true.

During these years the people of Israel continued to ignore the Lord. They trusted in their wealth and power, not in the Lord their God, and they kept committing crimes against the poor and the weak.

A few years after the birth of Jezreel, Hosea and Gomer had another child, and the Lord spoke to Hosea again.

"Name the girl Lo-Ruhamah," he said. "Call her 'Not Pitied' because I won't show pity to Israel anymore."

The girl's name was another sign of what the Lord was going to do. He was going to send disaster to Israel. And when disaster struck, he wouldn't pity the people and save them from their enemies.

Then Hosea and Gomer had a third child, and the Lord said, "Name the boy Lo-Ammi (Not My People), for Israel is not my people, and I am not their God."

This name was the most terrible sign of all, for it meant that the Lord was going to separate himself from Israel. This was the worst thing that could happen to them.

Hosea went out and spoke to the Israelites. He showed them his three children and explained why they were called Jezreel, Lo-Ruhamah, and Lo-Ammi. He warned the people that God was going to judge them, but they paid no attention.

After their children were born, Hosea's wife, Gomer, was unfaithful to him. She broke their mar-

riage agreement and left Hosea to go after other men.

"My lovers give me everything I need," she said.

"She is not my wife!" said Hosea. "And I am not her husband!"

He divorced her and took away everything he had given to her.

The Lord told Hosea that the people of Israel were like Gomer. They were an unfaithful wife. They had rejected the Lord their God, leaving him to go after other gods.

Instead of trusting in the Lord, the Israelites worshiped Baal, the Phoenician god of storm and rain. The Phoenicians called Baal "husband of the land." The Israelites said that Baal gave them bread and water, wool and flax and oil—everything they needed.

So the Lord, the true husband of Israel, was going to divorce them. He was going to take away everything he had given to them.

Then one day the Lord said to Hosea, "Go, love the woman who has left you for someone else, just as I love Israel, even though they have run after other gods."

Hosea went out and brought Gomer back. She had fallen into slavery, and he had to pay a price to redeem her. In those days men who divorced their wives never went looking for them to bring them back. But Hosea was ready to love Gomer as God loved Israel.

This was a sign of what the Lord was going to do.

He was going to punish Israel by letting the people be carried into captivity. Then, someday in the future, he would bring them back, paying a price to redeem them.

Hosea told the Israelites about God's great love for them. The Lord God was so holy, so righteous, that he punished evil. And he was so loving that he would never completely destroy his people. God felt like the parent of a wicked, disobedient child, a child he loved with all his heart.

Hosea told the people how God was going to punish them for being unfaithful. And he told them how God loved them so much, he would never let them go.

In the future, said Hosea, there would be a new day of Jezreel. This time it would not be a day of judgment, but a day of planting. And in that future time the Lord would show pity and save his people. He would say to them, "You are my people, the children of the living God!"

The Lord promised that he would bring his people back to the land, and they would live happily together, like a faithful wife and a loving husband.

4

The Proud King Who Offended God

2 Kings 15; 2 Chronicles 26

TWO hundred years before the time of Amos and Hosea, the twelve tribes of Israel were united in one kingdom. Then the northern tribes broke away, and the people of God were divided into the two kingdoms of Israel and Judah.

The Northern Kingdom of Israel, with its capital at Samaria, was larger and richer than Judah. But Israel was troubled with assassinations of its kings and many changes of royal family.

The Southern Kingdom of Judah had one royal family, the family of David. The people of Judah were proud of their kings; they remembered God's promise that someone from David's family would always rule over them. They were also proud of the magnificent temple on top of Mount Zion, the highest hill in Jerusalem. The temple of Jerusalem was larger and more beautiful than the temple of Bethel, and God had promised that the temple would be his home on earth.

While Jeroboam II was king of Israel, Uzziah was king of Judah. Uzziah ruled for fifty-two years, and as long as he obeyed the Lord, everything went well for him.

Uzziah loved farming. He planted trees and vineyards, wheat and barley, and raised herds of cattle.

He equipped his army with spears and shields, helmets, body armor, bows and arrows, slings and stones. At the corners of the walls of Jerusalem, Uzziah built defense towers. Inside the towers he installed machines that could shoot arrows and throw stones at invaders.

The Lord gave Uzziah victory over the Philistines in the west, the Ammonites in the east, and the desert tribes in the south. The territory, wealth, and power of Judah grew greater, and Uzziah became famous. Uzziah became so famous and so successful, he became proud. Instead of remembering that everything he had came from the Lord, he forgot the Lord and tried to increase his own power.

One day Uzziah went into the holy place, the main room of the temple. He knew that only priests

were allowed to burn incense on the golden altar in the holy place, but he was determined to take priestly power for himself.

Azariah the high priest saw Uzziah enter the sanctuary. He followed him, and a crowd of eighty priests walked behind.

"Uzziah!" cried the priests. "You know you're not supposed to do this. Only the priests of the Lord are allowed to burn incense on the golden altar. Leave the holy place at once! You have offended God!"

Uzziah stood still, with the incense burner in his hand. He refused to leave. He raged at Azariah and the other priests. How dare they tell the king what to do!

Suddenly the priests saw white spots breaking out on Uzziah's forehead—spots of leprosy, a dreadful skin disease. Everyone with leprosy was considered unclean and had to stay away from holy places and healthy people.

The priests made Uzziah leave the temple. He didn't argue, but went out quietly, for he realized that the Lord was punishing him, and he was afraid.

For the rest of his life Uzziah was sick with leprosy. He never entered the temple again. He never went anywhere, but stayed inside his house while his son Jotham ruled the kingdom.

When Uzziah died, his body was buried in a separate place, away from the royal tombs of the other kings of Judah.

5

Isaiah Meets the Holy God of Israel

Isaiah 6

IN the year that King Uzziah died, a young man named Isaiah had a vision of the Lord in the temple.

Isaiah saw the Lord, the heavenly King, sitting on his throne high in the holy place. The Lord's royal robe flowed over the floor, filling the sanctuary. Around him stood fiery creatures with six wings called seraphs. The bright seraphs called to each other, saying,

> Holy, holy, holy is the Lord of Hosts!
> The whole earth is full of his glory!

At the sound of their voices, the foundation of the temple shook. A cloud began to fill the sanctuary, and Isaiah was afraid.

"How miserable I am!" he cried. "I'm lost! For I'm a man of sinful, unclean lips, and I live among sinful people. Yet with my own eyes I have seen the King, the Lord of power and might."

Isaiah thought he would die because the sight of the holy God of Israel was too much for human eyes.

Then one of the seraphs picked up a pair of tongs from the altar of incense. He took a red-hot coal with the tongs and flew toward Isaiah.

"See!" said the seraph, as he touched the fiery coal to Isaiah's mouth, "this coal from the holy altar has touched your lips. Now your sin is forgiven and you are clean."

Then Isaiah heard the voice of the Lord saying,

Whom shall I send?
Who will be our messenger?

"Here I am!" cried Isaiah. "Send me!"

The Lord said, "Go to the people and tell them what I say to you. If they understand, they'll turn from their wicked ways and be changed. They'll be saved; they'll become healthy again. But it won't happen. The people will refuse to listen to you. They'll look, but they won't see. They'll hear, but they won't understand. The more you prophesy, the more stubborn they'll become."

"How long will this go on, Lord?" asked Isaiah.

"Until their cities are completely ruined!" answered the Lord. "Until their houses are empty! Until the land is deserted! For I'm going to drive the people out of the land. Yet, someday in the future a few of them will return. They'll rise up again like a new tree growing from the roots of an old stump."

For the rest of his life Isaiah prophesied to the kings and people of Judah. He spoke to them in the temple, in the palace, and in the streets of Jerusalem.

Although most people ignored Isaiah's messages, some disciples gathered around him and listened to his teachings. Isaiah was a humble man who became a great prophet.

The Song of the Vineyard

2 Kings 15; 2 Chronicles 27; Isaiah 1—5

U ZZIAH's son Jotham ruled Judah for sixteen years. He rebuilt the walls of Jerusalem and constructed fortresses in the countryside to defend the kingdom.

Jotham obeyed the Lord, and the Lord gave him victory over the Ammonites. But Jotham didn't destroy the pagan altars where the people of Judah worshiped idols.

The rulers, nobles, merchants, and landowners of Judah were like their cousins in the kingdom of Israel. They lied and cheated in order to increase their

33

wealth, and they bribed judges to win cases against poor people. They didn't care about the teachings of the Lord.

In those days Isaiah began to prophesy in Jerusalem. He said, "Hear the word of the Lord! The Lord says,

> I raised children,
>> but now they rebel against me!
>
> Even an ox knows its owner;
>> a donkey recognizes its master.
>
> But you know nothing;
>> my people are stupid!"

Isaiah warned that the Lord hated the people's empty religion and their crimes against the poor. The Lord was going to judge them. Unless they changed their wicked ways, enemies would invade the land and conquer them. But if they worshiped the Lord their God and obeyed his commandments, they would be saved.

"Listen!" cried Isaiah. "Hear what the Lord says to you:

> Come, let us reason together.
>
> Though your sins are like scarlet,
>> they will become as white as snow.
> Though they are as red as crimson,
>> they will be like sheeps' wool.

If you will just obey your God,
    you will eat the fruit of the land.
But if you rebel against him,
    you will taste the edge of your enemy's sword!"

Isaiah told the people a story called "The Song of the Vineyard." It was a parable, a simple story with a hidden message.

In this parable, the Lord is the farmer, and his people are the vineyard.

"Now let me sing about my friend," said Isaiah. "I'll tell you about his love for his vineyard.

"My friend had a vineyard. He owned a field on a fertile hillside.

"He dug the ground and cleared away the stones. He planted it with the finest grapevines. In the mid-

dle of the field he built a watchtower, and he dug out a grape press for making wine.

"My friend expected his vineyard to produce good, sweet grapes. But it yielded only worthless, sour ones!

"And now, you who live in Jerusalem, you people of Judah—the farmer asks you to judge between him and his vineyard.

"What else could he have done for his vineyard? What did he fail to do? He expected it to produce good grapes. Why did it yield worthless ones instead?

"Now I'll tell you what my friend is going to do with his vineyard. He'll take away its hedge, so animals will come and graze on it. He'll knock down its walls, so trespassers will trample on it.

"He'll make it a wasteland. No one will prune it or weed it. Thorns and briars will grow over it. He'll even order the clouds to send no rain on it!

"For the vineyard of the Lord is the twelve tribes of Israel. And the people of Judah are the plant that he chose.

"He expected justice, but he found violence. He looked for righteousness, but he heard only the cry of the poor!"

Three Signs of Hope

2 Kings 15—16; 2 Chronicles 28; Isaiah 7—8, 10, 17, 28

THE Lord gave Isaiah messages of judgment, but he also gave him three signs of hope for the future.

The first sign of hope was the name of Isaiah's oldest son. When the child was born, the Lord told him to name the boy Shear-Jashub, which meant "A remnant will return."

Isaiah took the child with him as he preached. When the people saw Shear-Jashub, they were reminded that the Lord was going to judge them, but someday he would bring them back to the land.

At this time the little kingdom of Judah was one of the few nations still independent of the Assyrian Empire. A soldier in the Assyrian army had seized power and become king. He called himself Tiglath-Pileser III. Tiglath-Pileser expanded his kingdom and built up a great empire, with its capital at Nineveh, on the Tigris River.

For the next two hundred years the kings of Assyria led mighty armies across the lands of the ancient Near East, conquering, killing, looting, and destroying the small nations that lay in their path.

When Tiglath-Pileser threatened the kingdom of Israel, Menahem ordered each of the rich men to pay fifty pieces of silver. Menahem collected thirty-eight tons of silver to give as tribute to the king of Assyria.

Tiglath-Pileser took the tribute and left without attacking Israel. But every year after that, the kings of Israel had to pay tribute to the king of Assyria. Menahem's son Pekahiah, and Pekah, who became king after him, were vassals, subjects of the great king.

Then Rezin, king of Damascus, plotted with some other Aramean kings to rebel against the Assyrians. He convinced King Pekah of Israel to join him. Then Rezin and Pekah tried to bring King Jotham of Judah into their plans.

Jotham refused to cooperate. Since Judah was still independent, he had nothing to gain by joining the rebellion. When Jotham's son Ahaz became king, he also refused.

This made Pekah and Rezin angry. They prepared to attack Judah and replace Ahaz with a king of their own choice.

One day a messenger arrived at Ahaz's palace in Jerusalem. "The Arameans are in Israel!" he cried.

This meant that Rezin's army had joined Pekah's army. Both forces would soon invade Judah. Ahaz and his officials were so frightened, they trembled like trees in the forest when the wind blows.

The Lord sent Isaiah to speak to Ahaz. Isaiah took his son Shear-Jashub and went out to the place where the city water supply was stored. A good water supply would be necessary in case the enemy attacked and besieged Jerusalem. If they surrounded the city and cut off all food and water sup-

plies, the people inside the city would be at their mercy. A siege could cause great suffering.

Isaiah found Ahaz inspecting the water supply. "Listen!" he said. "Don't be afraid of Rezin and Pekah. They're just smoking torches. Their fire has already been put out. The Lord says their plans will fail. Five or six years from now Pekah's whole kingdom will disappear. But here's a warning for you, Ahaz. If you don't trust in the Lord, you won't survive either."

Ahaz paid no attention to Isaiah. He was a wicked man who worshiped idols on the hills, at the high places, and under every green and shady tree in the kingdom. He had made metal images of Baal, the Canaanite god, and he had set the images up for the people to worship. He had even sacrificed one of his own sons as a burnt offering to the idols.

A little while later the Lord sent Isaiah to speak to Ahaz again.

"Ask the Lord your God for a sign," said Isaiah. "Make it as deep as the underworld of the dead, or as high as heaven. Ask for anything at all!"

"No," answered Ahaz. "I won't put the Lord to the test."

"Listen, king!" said Isaiah. "You're already testing the Lord's patience! Very well, the Lord himself will give you a sign—the sign of Immanuel. A maiden will give birth to a son, and she will call him Immanuel (God is with us.) Before the child is grown, your enemies will be destroyed."

This was the second sign of hope. The Lord was

40

promising to send a royal prince from the family of David to save his people from their enemies.

Isaiah realized that Ahaz didn't believe God's promises, so he warned, "The Lord is going to humble the royal family. A few years from now he'll call the Egyptians and the Assyrians to come and fight each other in your land. Then the Lord will shave Judah with a razor blade hired from Assyria. He'll remove the hair from the head and the whole body, not just the beard. He'll use the king of Assyria to destroy your kingdom."

But again Ahaz ignored Isaiah's message. Instead of turning to the Lord, he offered sacrifices to idols.

"The gods of Damascus helped the Arameans," said Ahaz to himself. "If I sacrifice to them, maybe they'll help me, too!"

Then Ahaz collected the equipment from the Lord's temple and smashed it. He sealed the temple doors shut so no one could go in, and he told the people to worship other gods.

The Lord punished Ahaz by letting him fall into the hands of his enemies. Pekah and Rezin came with their armies and attacked Judah. They captured many prisoners and killed a hundred and twenty units of Ahaz's soldiers.

During the attack, Isaiah reminded the people of Jerusalem and Judah that the Lord was still in control.

"Rezin's kingdom will disappear," he said. "Damascus will become a heap of ruins. And Pekah's kingdom will be like a fruit tree that's picked clean. Nothing will be left of Israel but two or three berries on the top branches."

Although the people heard Isaiah's message, they didn't understand. They didn't turn to the Lord.

Then Isaiah and his wife, who was also a prophet, had another son.

"Call him Maher-shalal, Hash-baz," said the Lord. (Maher-shalal, Hash-baz means "Easy pickings, Fast loot.") "Before the boy can say 'Dada' or 'Mama,' the king of Assyria will come and carry off the riches of Damascus and Samaria as loot."

Maher-shalal, Hash-baz's name was the third sign of hope. Like the names Shear-Jashub and Immanuel, this sign was a promise that the Lord would save his people.

Isaiah wrote down the Lord's words and said to his disciples, "These words will be a witness for the future. When people read what I've written, they'll know that God is faithful, for someday God will fulfill his promises."

The Fall of Samaria

2 Kings 16—17; 2 Chronicles 28

AHAZ was so afraid of Pekah and Rezin that he asked Tiglath-Pileser to help him. He took silver and gold from his palace, from the temple, and from the mansions of his nobles and sent it as tribute to the king of Assyria.

"Ahaz is your devoted servant," said his messengers to Tiglath-Pileser. "Come and rescue him!"

Tiglath-Pileser accepted Ahaz's tribute, and he sent his army to attack Pekah and Rezin.

First the Assyrians marched to Damascus, where they destroyed fields and gardens and wiped out towns and villages. They brutally murdered hundreds of Arameans, including King Rezin, and they carried eight hundred prisoners back to Nineveh.

Damascus became a heap of ruins, as Isaiah had prophesied. Rezin's kingdom disappeared; it was swallowed up by the great Assyrian Empire.

Then Tiglath-Pileser turned his forces against the kingdom of Israel. He conquered all of its territory except the hilltop city of Samaria and the mountains around it. He plotted with an Israelite named Hoshea to assassinate Pekah and then he set Hoshea up as the new king.

By the time the Assyrian army withdrew, Israel was ruined. It was like a fruit tree, picked clean except for the city of Samaria. God's word was coming true.

The kingdom of Judah was safe, but at a price. Ahaz was now a vassal, subject to the Assyrian king. He went to Damascus to meet Tiglath-Pileser, to bow down before him and show his loyalty.

While he was there, Ahaz was impressed with the great altar at Damascus. He sent a scale model and measurements to his priests in Jerusalem, telling them to make an exact copy of it. When he returned home, he moved the old altar of the Lord out of the way to make room for the new altar.

"Use this new altar for all the worship services," he said to the high priest. "Never mind about that old bronze altar of the Lord."

The high priest did as the king commanded.

Ahaz took the valuable bronze equipment from

the temple and sent it to Tiglath-Pileser. He encouraged the people of Judah to worship the gods of Assyria and kept the temple doors closed so they couldn't worship the Lord.

King Hoshea of Israel was less loyal to Assyria than Ahaz. A few years later, when Tiglath-Pileser died, Hoshea began to plot with the Egyptians against Shalmaneser, the new king of Assyria.

As soon as Shalmaneser found out about it, he ordered his officials to arrest Hoshea and put him in chains. Then he sent soldiers from the imperial army to attack the rebels.

The city of Samaria was so strong, the Israelites were able to hold out against the Assyrians for three years. During the siege Shalmaneser died, and King Sargon II continued the attack. Finally, the city fell.

The wealth of Samaria was carried off to Nin-

eveh. Sargon put his own officials in charge and made Samaria part of his empire. The Assyrians took thousands of prisoners. The wealthy men and women of Samaria suffered, and their mansions completely disappeared. Sargon forced them to settle in cities in faraway parts of the empire. They married men and women of foreign nations and nobody ever heard of them again.

The Assyrians sent people from other nations of the empire to take their place. It was official Assyrian policy to mix up the nationalities of the empire so the subjects would be loyal to Assyria.

At first the settlers didn't worship the Lord, and lions came and killed them. When Sargon heard about this, he ordered his officials to send an Israelite priest to Samaria to teach the new people the ways of the God of Israel. Sargon thought the god of each nation had power in his own land. But he didn't believe the Lord was greater than any other god.

The Israelite priest came and taught the people to worship the Lord. They worshiped him along with the god of the sky, the god of the underworld, and all the other gods they knew.

These people became known as Samaritans, and the territory of the old kingdom of Israel was known as Samaria. From now on, the name "Israel" meant the people of the Southern Kingdom and the few survivors in the north.

The prophecies of Amos and Hosea were coming true.

The Lord Defends Jerusalem

What Does the Lord Require?

Micah

DURING the years that Isaiah was prophesying in Jerusalem and Judah, the Lord sent another prophet to warn the people. This was Micah, a man from the village of Moresheth in the lowlands south of Jerusalem.

Micah warned the people of Jerusalem that the Lord would punish them as he had punished Samaria if they didn't change their way of living.

"The rich people plot to steal from the poor," he said. "The rulers mislead the people. The leaders of Israel hate justice. They twist everything that's right. They build Zion with blood; Jerusalem, with crime. They decide cases according to the bribes they receive. The priests interpret God's teachings for pay. The prophets say anything that makes them rich. And yet they all say, 'The Lord is with us! No evil can overcome us.'

"Therefore, the Lord says, 'Zion will become a plowed field. Jerusalem will be a pile of ruins. The mountain of the temple will go back to woodland.' For the Lord will punish you by letting foreign nations invade the land and conquer you."

Micah told the people of Judah that the Lord didn't care about fancy worship services and expensive offerings. What the Lord wanted from them was justice and righteousness.

"You ask what gift you should bring to the Lord," said Micah. "What sacrifice is great enough to take away your sin?

"You already know what is good; it has been explained to you, O man. For this is what the Lord requires, only this: *To do justice, to show kindness, and to walk humbly with your God.*"

Micah saw a vision of the future, when the Lord himself would reign in Jerusalem. Then the whole world would learn about the true God.

"In the days to come," Micah said,

"The mountain of the temple of the Lord
　　will be lifted higher than the hills.

The nations will stream to it;
　　great nations will come, and they will say,

'Come, let us go up to the mountain of the Lord,
　　to the temple of the God of Jacob.

He will teach us his ways,
　　and we will walk in his paths.

For his teaching goes out from Zion;
　　the word of the Lord comes from Jerusalem.' "

In his vision Micah saw everyone on earth living in peace.

"In those days," he said,

"The Lord will rule over many peoples;
　　he will judge between great nations.

They will hammer their swords into plowshares,
their spears into pruning hooks.

Nation will not lift sword against nation;
they won't prepare for war any more.

But each man will sit under his own vine and fig tree,
and no one will make him afraid."

Someday, said Micah, a wonderful new king would be born in the town of Bethlehem. He would rule over God's people. He would rule over the whole earth. He would be the one to bring peace to the world.

10

Hezekiah Reopens the Temple

2 Kings 18; 2 Chronicles 29—31

HEZEKIAH was the opposite of his father Ahaz. He obeyed the Lord and paid attention to the words of Isaiah and Micah. Hezekiah was one of Judah's best kings.

In the first month of the first year of his reign, while he was still a young man, Hezekiah threw open the doors of the temple. After he had the doors repaired, he called the priests and their helpers, the Levites, to meet with him.

"Listen to me!" said Hezekiah. "Our fathers left the Lord. They closed the temple and let the lamps in the holy place go out. They didn't burn incense or offer sacrifices to the Lord. That's why the Lord punished Judah and let our enemies defeat us. Now I'm going to ask the people to stop worshiping idols. I'm going to ask them to return to the Lord their God. Purify yourselves and the temple. Come, let's begin right now!"

The priests and the Levites worked for a whole week. They took the idols out of the temple and threw them into the city dump in the Kidron Valley outside the walls of Jerusalem.

They spent another week preparing the temple for worship. They set up the altar, replaced the furniture and equipment, relit the lamps, and offered incense on the golden altar in the holy place.

Then they reported to Hezekiah, "We've cleaned the whole temple and made it ready for worship. We brought back everything that Ahaz removed."

Hezekiah called the rulers of Jerusalem and asked them to come with him to the temple. They brought offerings for the Lord to take away the sins of the royal family and the nation.

Then they held a great service to rededicate the temple. The Levites sang psalms, the priests blew their silver trumpets, and the musicians played their stringed instruments while the people prayed to the Lord.

Hezekiah sent messengers to invite everyone to come to Jerusalem to celebrate the Passover. Passover was the great feast which reminded God's people how God had rescued them from slavery in

Egypt. Hezekiah wanted to make Passover a time for everyone to come together. He called all Israel, even the people in the territory of the old Northern Kingdom.

The king's messengers went to every village and town in the north, saying, "People of Israel! Return to the Lord, and he will be with you!"

But most of them laughed and made fun of Hezekiah. Only a few were humble enough to come to Jerusalem.

In Judah the power of God was working among the people. Almost everyone came to the temple for Passover. The priests and the Levites who hadn't been participating felt ashamed, and they came, too.

When the great crowd of men, women, and children arrived at the temple, Hezekiah prayed, "May the good Lord pardon everyone whose heart is ready to seek him!"

The people ate the special food Hezekiah had provided. Everyone in Jerusalem was filled with joy, for nothing so wonderful had happened since the days of King Solomon. They had such a good time, they stayed a second week.

Then Hezekiah sent the people through the land to smash the pagan altars and to destroy the idols.

He organized the priests in Jerusalem to lead regular worship services. He asked the people to bring offerings to support the priests and Levites, so they could be free to teach the people about the Lord.

The people brought the best of everything they had: gifts of grain, wine, oil, honey, sheep, and cattle.

Hezekiah and his officials were amazed at the size of the offerings, and they praised the Lord and his people.

"The people have brought more than we need!" said the high priest.

Hezekiah told the priests to prepare rooms in the temple to store the gifts.

Hezekiah did other things to encourage the people to follow the ways of the Lord. He told his scribes to write down proverbs and other sayings and to make copies on scrolls. They wrote down the teachings of Moses and the old stories of Abraham, Joshua, and

David—the whole wonderful story of God and his people.

Everything Hezekiah did was successful, for he was acting in the spirit of devotion to his God.

11

The Barefoot Prophet

2 Kings 18; Isaiah 18—20, 30—31

KING Hezekiah was wealthy and successful. The rulers of the neighboring states respected him and looked to him for leadership.

Then Sargon II died, and the vassal kings of the empire murmured rebellion. Pharaoh Shabaka, king of Egypt, invited Hezekiah to join him in a plot against Assyria. Hezekiah prepared to send ambassadors to Egypt to work on an agreement with his powerful neighbor.

Before the ambassadors left, Isaiah the prophet arrived at the palace with a message from the Lord.

"You're making alliances without consulting God!" warned Isaiah. "You're seeking safety in Egypt, not in the power of the Lord. Instead of trusting in him, you're putting your faith in war horses, in chariots, and in soldiers.

"The Egyptians are men, not gods. Their horses are flesh, not spirit. You're taking rich presents on the backs of donkeys, treasures on camels' humps— all to a worthless nation!

"Pharaoh's protection will shame you, for the Egyptians will prove to be useless. They'll bring you disgrace, not help. The Lord is going to stretch out his hand to make them stumble. When they fall, you'll go down with them."

Hezekiah ignored Isaiah's warning. He joined Shabaka in the plot and rebelled against the empire. He was sure that the Egyptians were powerful enough to resist the Assyrians.

Then the Lord said to Isaiah, "Go, take off the sackcloth you're wearing; remove the sandals from your feet."

Isaiah did as the Lord commanded. He walked through the streets of Jerusalem barefoot and naked, except for his loincloth. He became a sign to the people of the shame that was coming.

"Listen!" he said. "The king of Assyria will lead captives from Egypt. All of them, young and old, will be naked and barefoot. When that happens, you'll be frightened and ashamed, because you trusted in the Egyptians; you bragged about their power. Everyone who sees their disgrace will say,

'Look what happened to the people we trusted in, to the ones we ran to for safety. How can we escape the same fate?'

For three years Isaiah prophesied disaster while the people of Judah rejoiced. They were certain that the rebellion would succeed. The Edomites, the Moabites, and the Philistines refused to pay tribute. The Philistine cities broke out in anti-Assyrian riots.

Sennacherib, the son of Sargon, was too busy putting down revolts in the eastern part of his empire to bother about Egypt and Judah and their neighbors in the west. It seemed that the military leaders of Judah had achieved peace and freedom through clever politics and military strength. No one paid any attention to the barefoot prophet who wandered through Jerusalem speaking of shame and defeat.

12

The Miracle of the Sundial

2 Kings 20; 2 Chronicles 32; Isaiah 38—39

DURING the third year of the rebellion King Hezekiah became ill. He had a tumor that was so diseased, he almost died.

Isaiah went to see him and said, "This is what the Lord says, 'Put your affairs in order, for you're going to die.'"

Hezekiah turned his face to the wall and prayed, "O Lord, remember how faithfully I've served you. I've always tried to do what you wanted me to do." And he cried long and bitterly.

While Isaiah was on his way out of the palace, the

Lord said to him, "Go back to Hezekiah and tell him that I've heard his prayer and I've seen his tears. I'll heal him; I'll add fifteen years to his life. I'll save him and this city from the power of the king of Assyria, for the sake of my honor and the promise I made to David. In three days Hezekiah will be well enough to go to the temple."

Isaiah turned around and went back to the king's room. He said to the king's servants, "Make a paste of dried figs and put it on the king's tumor, and he'll recover."

Then Isaiah told Hezekiah what the Lord had said.

Hezekiah asked, "What's the sign to tell me that these words will come true?"

On the roof of the palace was a sundial that Hezekiah's father, Ahaz, had made. It told the time by the position of the sun's shadow.

"This will be the sign," answered Isaiah. "The Lord will move the shadow on the steps of Ahaz's sundial. Then you will know that the Lord will do as he has said. Do you want him to move the shadow ten steps forward or ten steps backward?"

"Backward," answered Hezekiah. "That would be a greater miracle."

Isaiah prayed to the Lord, and the Lord made the shadow on the sundial move ten steps backward.

The news of Hezekiah's healing and the miracle of the sundial reached all the way to the opposite end of the vast Assyrian Empire, all the way to Merodach-Baladan, ruler of Babylon. Merodach-Baladan was also rebelling against the Assyrians. He decided to send messengers with letters and presents for Hezekiah.

Hezekiah welcomed the visitors from Babylon. He showed them his military equipment and the wealth in his storerooms. He had great treasures of gold and silver, spices, perfumes, and jewels, as well as grain, wine, and olive oil.

Hezekiah was startled when Isaiah came to him later and demanded, "Where did these men come from, and what did they say?"

"They came from a far country," he answered. "From Babylon."

"What have they seen in your palace?"

"Everything. I showed them all my treasures."

"Now hear the word of the Lord!" said Isaiah. "The time is coming when everything in your

palace—all the treasures stored up by your ancestors—will be carried off to Babylon. And some of your own descendants will be taken captive to serve a foreign king."

"Well," answered Hezekiah. "Your message makes me feel better." He was thinking to himself, "So what? At least there will be peace and freedom for the rest of my life."

13

Sennacherib Insults the Lord

2 Kings 18; 2 Chronicles 32; Isaiah 22, 29, 36

MERODACH-Baladan kept the Assyrian army pinned down in the east for several years, but finally Sennacherib regained control. Then the Assyrian King turned his forces westward, toward Egypt and Judah.

Hezekiah prepared for a long siege. He sent some men to cut off the water supply outside the city. They blocked up all the springs and channels in the countryside, saying, "Why should the Assyrians find water when they arrive?"

Jerusalem's water came from Gihon spring,

which flowed down a channel to a pool just outside the city walls. Hezekiah ordered his workers to dig a long, winding tunnel underneath the city, so the water would flow into the Pool of Siloam, inside the walls.

While some men dug through the rock with pickaxes, others repaired the city walls and strengthened them with defense towers.

Hezekiah checked his storerooms, counted the weapons and armor, and ordered more to be made.

Then the prophet Isaiah came to him and said, "You made all these preparations to defend the city against the Assyrians, but you forgot your Maker! You won't need your water tunnel, your walls and towers, your swords and arrows. The Lord can defend Jerusalem. He'll scatter your enemies like dust. They'll vanish like a dream in the morning. The soldiers who attack Jerusalem will be like a hungry man who dreams about a good dinner and then wakes up with an empty stomach. They'll be like a thirsty man who dreams of drinking and wakes up exhausted with a dry throat."

Soon after this Sennacherib's army entered Judah. They captured all the towns west of Jerusalem except Lachish, a fortress that guarded the way to the city.

When Hezekiah realized that the Egyptians weren't going to help him, he sent a message to Sennacherib.

"I've done wrong," he said. "Please withdraw your troops, and I'll pay whatever tribute you demand."

Sennacherib asked for a ton of gold and ten tons of silver.

Hezekiah stripped the gold from the door of the temple, took all the silver he could find in the storerooms of the temple and the palace, and sent everything to Sennacherib in Lachish.

Still the Assyrians didn't leave. So Hezekiah ordered his military commanders to take charge of the city, and he told the people of Jerusalem to meet him in the city square.

"Be strong and brave," he said to them. "Don't be afraid. Don't tremble at the king of Assyria or his army, for we have more power than they do. Sennacherib has only human power, while we have the Lord our God fighting for us!"

The people felt encouraged by Hezekiah's words.

When Hezekiah returned to his palace, he heard that Sennacherib was sending three officials with a message for him and the people of Jerusalem.

Hezekiah sent three of his own officials to meet them. When they arrived, one of the Assyrians said, "Hear the words of the great king, the emperor of Assyria! He wants to know what makes you so sure of yourselves. Do you think the empty words of your king are as strong as our army? First you trusted in the Egyptians. That did you no good. Now you're trusting in the Lord your God. When your king says your God will save you, he's condemning you to die!"

Hezekiah's officials answered, "Please don't say these things to us in Hebrew, for the people on the wall are listening. Please speak to us in Aramaic."

The officials knew Aramaic, the international language, but the common people understood only Hebrew.

The Assyrian official looked up at the crowd on the city wall. "Do you think the great king has sent us to speak only to you and your king?" he asked. "I'm here to speak to those people up there, too. They're going to suffer! We'll besiege your city until they die of hunger and thirst!"

Then the Assyrian stood up and shouted loudly in Hebrew, "Hear the words of the great king, the emperor of Assyria! Don't let Hezekiah talk you into trusting your God. He can't save you! Surrender to us! Don't suffer through a long siege. If you surrender now, we'll take good care of you. The great Sennacherib will send you to another land, a good land full of vineyards and fields, with grain, olive oil, and honey. Obey Sennacherib, and you'll live. Obey Hezekiah, and you'll die!

"Don't trust in the Lord!" he shouted. "Remember, none of the gods of the other nations could save their people from our power—not one! So what makes you think your God can save you? No one can defeat the great Sennacherib!"

The people on the wall didn't answer, for Hezekiah had ordered them to be silent.

Hezekiah's officials tore their clothes in grief. Then they returned to the palace to report the terrible things they had heard.

The Lord Defends Jerusalem

2 Kings 19; 2 Chronicles 32; Isaiah 10, 22, 37

WHEN Hezekiah heard how the Assyrians had insulted the Lord, he tore his clothes and put on sackcloth as a sign of mourning. He told his officials to take a message to Isaiah, and then he went to the temple to pray.

"O Lord God!" cried Hezekiah. "Ruler of all the kingdoms of the world, Creator of heaven and earth! Hear my prayer! Pay attention to the insults of these Assyrians against the living God! Sennacherib brags about how he has destroyed many nations and burned up their gods—worthless images made by human hands. O Lord God, rescue us from the power of the Assyrians, so all the nations of the earth will know that you, Lord, are the only God!"

While Hezekiah was praying in the temple, his officials went to Isaiah and said, "This is a day of disgrace! The king of Assyria has insulted the living God! May the Lord your God punish him! Pray to the Lord to save Jerusalem!"

"Hear what the Lord says," answered Isaiah. "Don't be afraid of what Sennacherib's officials say. Their words won't come true. Sennacherib brags about his great power, but he's just a club in the hand of the Lord. He's like an ax taking more credit than the man who uses it! The Lord has finished punishing Judah, and now he's going to punish Sennacherib. He'll strike Sennacherib's army with disease. Then he'll send Sennacherib back to his own country, where he'll die by the sword!"

When Isaiah finished speaking to Hezekiah's servants, he went to see the king.

"The Lord God of Israel has heard your prayer," he said. "Listen to what the Lord says to Sennacherib:

Jerusalem despises you, king of Assyria!
This city laughs at you behind your back!

Do you know whom you have insulted?
Whom you have raised your voice against?

Against the Holy One of Israel!
You have insulted the Lord!

You're impressed with your own power;
  you brag about your victories.

Don't you know?
  Hasn't anyone told you?

This was all planned long ago.
  The Lord decided these things would happen;
    now he's carrying out his plan!

You were playing your part
  when you destroyed cities;
you were the Lord's instrument
  to punish the nations.

Now it's time for the Lord to punish you
  for raving against him,
    for insulting him.

He'll put his ring through your nose,
his bit between your teeth,

and lead you home like an animal,
to return the same way you came!

"The Lord will save Jerusalem!" said Isaiah. "The king of Assyria won't even enter the city. He won't shoot a single arrow against it. The Lord will defend Jerusalem for the sake of the promises he made to his servant David."

That night the angel of the Lord went to the place where the Assyrian army was camped. The angel struck down two hundred units of fighting men. Every single man, both officers and ordinary soldiers, died of disease.

Sennacherib returned to Nineveh without his great army. He never came back to Judah. And a few years later, as he was entering the temple of his god, two of his own sons killed him with their swords. They ran away to the land of Armenia, and another son, Esarhaddon, became king.

When the people of the empire heard how the Lord had saved Jerusalem and punished Sennacherib, they brought offerings for the Lord and gifts for Hezekiah.

Hezekiah lived fifteen more years, as the Lord had promised. He enjoyed wealth and honor, and the land enjoyed peace and freedom.

The Prince of Peace

Isaiah 9, 11—12, 27

ISAIAH brought messages of hope for the future of God's people. He told them about a wonderful king who would come from the family of David. The Spirit of the Lord would be on this king, and he would rule with wisdom and power.

Isaiah said,

> The people who walked in darkness
>   have seen a great light.
> They rejoice in the presence of the Lord,
>   like farmers celebrating the harvest.

For a great weight has been
        lifted from their shoulders;
    the Lord has broken the power
        that was burdening them.

He has destroyed the weapons of war;
    he has burned military uniforms and equip-
    ment.

    For a child is born for us;
        a son is given for us.

And the government will be upon his shoulders;
        and he will be called
            Wonderful Counselor,
            Mighty God,
            Eternal Father,
            Prince of Peace!

He will rule the whole world
    in a peace that never ends;
he will reign with justice and righteousness
    forever and ever!

When the Prince of Peace comes, explained Isaiah, his kingdom will include all living creatures, both wild animals and tame.
In that peaceable kingdom

The wolf will live with the lamb;
    the panther will lie down with the young goat;
the calf and the lion cub will eat together,
    and a little child will lead them.

The cow and the bear will make friends;
    their children will lie down together;
        the lion will eat straw like the ox.

The baby will play above the cobra's hole;
    the child will put his hand into the nest of
    snakes;
        and no one will harm them,
            no one will be hurt
                on God's holy mountain.

And the land will be filled with the knowledge of God
    as the waters fill up the sea!

In that day, said Isaiah, the Lord will restore his people. He'll bring back the remnant of Israel and Judah from all the places where they have scattered. He'll make a dry path for them across the ocean. He'll lead them home.

Then God's people will give thanks to him. They'll trust him, and they'll tell the whole world how he saved them.

In that day, there will be a new "Song of the Vineyard." The Lord will watch over his vineyard day and night. He'll keep all invaders out. He'll destroy every thorn and briar. He'll order the clouds to send rain.

Then the vine will put forth new branches, and God's people will grow and blossom. They'll fill the whole world with wonderful fruit!

Visions of
Disaster

16

The Lord Forgives a Wicked King

2 Kings 21; 2 Chronicles 33

MANASSEH, the son of Hezekiah, became king when he was only twelve years old. He reigned for fifty-five years, longer than any other king of Judah. During his reign the Assyrians were at the height of their power. They defeated the Egyptians, just as Isaiah had prophesied.

Manasseh remained loyal to the Assyrians. He paid them tribute and urged the people of Judah to follow Assyrian customs. He encouraged them to worship the sun, the moon, the planets, and the stars of the zodiac. He set up altars for astrologers in the courtyard of the temple, and he encouraged fortunetelling and witchcraft.

Manasseh behaved more like his wicked grandfather, Ahaz, than like his good father, Hezekiah. He told the people to rebuild the pagan altars that Hezekiah had smashed, so they could worship Baal, the Phoenician god of storm and rain. He set up pillars to worship Asherah, the goddess of love and war. He even put a pagan altar and image of Asherah inside the temple of the Lord.

Manasseh led the people of Judah into worse sins than the sins of the pagan people who lived around them. He sacrificed some of his own sons as burnt offerings to idols, and he told the people of Judah to do the same.

The Lord was furious because of Manasseh's crimes. He sent prophets to warn the king that he was going to send disaster to Jerusalem and Judah.

"The disaster will be terrible!" cried the prophets. "The ears of those who hear about it will tingle. The Lord will punish the kingdom of Judah as he punished the kingdom of Israel. He'll wipe Jerusalem clean, like a dish that's dried out and turned upside down."

Manasseh ignored all these warnings; he ordered the people not to listen to the prophets. He persecuted them, killing so many innocent people like Isaiah and Micah that Jerusalem was full of their blood.

The Lord punished Manasseh by sending the

Assyrian army to invade Judah. The Assyrian commanders took Manasseh and stuck hooks into him and bound him in bronze chains and carried him off as a prisoner.

Manasseh suffered terribly, and as he suffered, his heart began to change. He humbled himself and turned to the Lord and admitted his crimes. He begged the Lord for mercy, for he knew that the Lord was kind and good.

Although Manasseh was one of the worst sinners who ever lived, the Lord listened to his prayers and forgave him. He brought Manasseh back to Jerusalem and let him rule again. Manasseh knew that this was a sign that the

Lord had really forgiven him, that the Lord was truly God.

In the last years of his life Manasseh tried to live according to the commandments and teachings of the Lord. He took the idols out of the temple and threw them into the city dump. He tore down the pagan altars and repaired the altar of the Lord. He tried his best to undo all the harm he had done, and he encouraged the people to turn back to the Lord their God.

17

Zephaniah Warns Judah

2 Kings 21; 2 Chronicles 33; Zephaniah

ALTHOUGH Manasseh changed his heart and turned to the Lord, the wicked things he had done earlier in his life influenced many people, including his own family. When Manasseh died, his son Amon became king. Amon was worse than Manasseh had ever been. He sinned greatly against the Lord by worshiping idols and disobeying the Lord's commandments.

After two years, some of Amon's officials plotted against him and assassinated him in his palace.

The common people were so outraged, they turned on the assassins and killed them and crowned Amon's little eight-year-old son Josiah as king.

In the early years of Josiah's reign, the Lord sent a new prophet to Judah, a nobleman named Zephaniah. He was the first prophet to appear since Manasseh had massacred so many prophets years before.

Zephaniah announced to the king and the people that the day of the Lord was coming. It would be a day of judgment on all nations, he said. The Lord was sending warnings to the people of Judah so they would humble themselves, turn back to the Lord, and change their way of living.

"The Lord is coming to judge the whole world!" cried Zephaniah. "Hear the word of the Lord. He says:

I'll sweep everything completely away—
    the people and the animals,
        the birds and the fish!

I'll strike Judah
    and all the people of Jerusalem!

I'll wipe out Baal
    and every trace of foreign gods!

I'll destroy the star-worshipers
    and the people who pretend to pray to me
        while they're calling on idols!

I'll attack the ones who have left me,
    the people who have looked for other gods!

"Be silent in the presence of the Lord God!" cried Zephaniah, "for the day of the Lord is coming soon.

"He'll punish the officials who are giving bad advice to our young king. He'll strike down the people who copy the customs of the Assyrians.

"When the Lord comes, he'll punish the rulers who misuse their authority and the wealthy who misuse their riches. He'll punish those who laugh at him and say, 'The Lord has no power to do good or evil.'"

The day of the Lord is near;
It's coming soon.

It will be a bitter day,
a day of anger,
a day of trouble,
a day of ruin,
a day of darkness,
a day of battle!

"Before that day comes, seek the Lord! Seek justice! Seek humility! Then perhaps the Lord will save you!"

Like the prophets Amos, Hosea, Micah, and Isaiah, Zephaniah warned the people of God's judgment and also brought them messages of hope.

Someday, said Zephaniah, the whole world will turn to the Lord. Everyone will pray to him, serve him, and worship him.

In that day God's people will be poor and humble. They will be a holy people, honest and peaceful. The Lord will save them, take care of them, and give them everything they need.

In that day, said Zephaniah, the people will sing with joy.

Shout for joy, O Daughter Zion;
sing with happiness, O Israel!

For the Lord will forgive you;
he'll defeat your enemies.

The Lord is with you;
    don't be afraid.

The Lord will rejoice over you, with gladness;
    he'll renew you in his love.
He'll sing joyfully because of you,
    with holiday music!

"And someday," said Zephaniah, "the Lord will gather his people and bring them home. He'll make his people famous among all the nations of the world. And then the whole earth will praise the people of God."

18

Josiah Seeks the Lord

2 Kings 22—23; 2 Chronicles 34—35

DURING the reigns of Manasseh and Amon, the people of Judah had forgotten the Lord their God. But now some of them, including King Josiah, listened to Zephaniah and began to seek the Lord. In the eighth year of his reign, when he was sixteen years old, Josiah turned to the Lord. And four years later he began to get rid of idols.

Josiah had many good advisers who were faithful to the Lord. With their help he began to clean the temple in Jerusalem. He asked the people of

Judah to bring silver to help pay for repairs to the temple. Everyone wanted to help, even the people who lived in the territory of the old Northern Kingdom.

One day in the eighteenth year of his reign, Josiah sent Shaphan, the royal scribe, to the temple. He told Shaphan, "Go to Hilkiah, the high priest, and tell him to melt down the silver that the people have donated. Tell him to use it to pay for carpenters, builders, and masons, and to buy timber and stones to repair the temple."

Shaphan did as the king commanded, and Hilkiah the high priest melted down the silver and used it to pay for the temple repairs.

While Hilkiah was taking the silver out of the storerooms, he made a surprising discovery. He found an old book-scroll that had been hidden away during the days of Manasseh and Amon. On the scroll was written part of the law of Moses. It told how God's people should live and what would happen if they didn't obey the Lord.

"I've found the book of the law in the temple!" said Hilkiah, and he gave it to Shaphan.

Shaphan took the scroll and read it. Then he rushed to the palace to see the king.

When he arrived before the king, Shaphan said, "We've done everything you commanded. We've taken the silver from the temple and handed it over to the men in charge of the repairs. Now, see what I've brought—a scroll that Hilkiah gave me!"

Shaphan unrolled the scroll and read it aloud to the king. He read the words that said how the Lord wanted his people to live, how they should love God and one another, be kind and honest, and never worship idols.

The Lord had made a special agreement—a covenant—with his people. According to the covenant, if the people obeyed God's teaching, he would give them everything they needed. He would let them stay in the land forever, and he would be their God. But if they disobeyed God's teaching, he would let their enemies defeat them, and he would drive them out of the land he had given them.

As Josiah listened to these words, he became so upset, he tore his clothes and began to cry. Then he ordered Shaphan and Hilkiah to go and consult the Lord.

"Find out more about the teachings on this scroll," he said. "The Lord must be very angry indeed, for we haven't been living as we should!"

At the king's command, Hilkiah and Shaphan went with three other officials to see Huldah, who was a prophetess and the wife of a temple official. They told her what had happened, and she consulted the Lord.

"Hear the word of the Lord God of Israel!" said Huldah. "Go back to the king and tell him that the Lord is going to punish Jerusalem and all its people, as it says on the scroll, for God's people have rejected him. They have worshiped other

92

gods, and his anger is poured out on Jerusalem!

"Tell King Josiah that the Lord says to him: 'I've heard your prayer. I've seen how you humbled yourself. For this reason, I won't punish Jerusalem during your lifetime. Your eyes won't see the terrible disaster I'm going to send."

Then Josiah's officials returned to the palace and told the King what Huldah had said.

Josiah called together the leaders of Judah and Jerusalem and went with them to the temple. There they met all the people—rich and poor, young and old. As Josiah read aloud to them from the scroll, everyone listened to God's teaching. Men, women, and children heard how the

Lord wanted them to live and what would happen if they disobeyed his commandments.

Josiah promised to obey the Lord and to live according to his teachings. The people agreed to do the same. Then Josiah told them to get rid of all their idols, to burn them in the rubbish heap in the Kidron Valley.

The people did as Josiah commanded. They stopped worshiping foreign gods and the stars of the zodiac.

Josiah sent away all the fortune-tellers, and he outlawed the use of charms and magic. He destroyed the pagan altars and idols in Jerusalem and Judah.

Three hundred years earlier a prophet had told King Jeroboam I of Israel that the altar of Bethel would be destroyed by a king named Josiah. Now these words came true. Josiah went up to Bethel and tore down the temple. He broke up the great altar and pounded it to dust, and he burned the idols and images of Asherah.

In these days the power of Assyria was so weak that Josiah was able to take over the territory of Samaria (the old kingdom of Israel). He tore down the pagan temples and struck down the pagan priests in all the cities and towns. Then he ordered all holy places outside Jerusalem to be destroyed, because they tempted the people to worship idols. He told all the priests of the Lord who were scattered through the land to come and serve at the temple in Jerusalem.

Then Josiah ordered, "Let's celebrate the Passover in honor of the Lord our God!"

He donated thousands of lambs, goats, and bulls from his own herds and flocks, and his officials and the nobles of Judah did the same.

The people of Judah and Israel came to celebrate the Passover in Jerusalem. It was even more wonderful than the Passover that they had celebrated when Hezekiah was king. No Passover like this had been celebrated since the days of the Judges, five hundred years earlier.

· And no king like Josiah had ever ruled in Judah, for Josiah served the Lord with all his heart and mind and strength, and he obeyed all the teachings of the Lord his God.

19

God Sends Jeremiah

Jeremiah 1—6, 16

JEREMIAH was a young man about the same age as Josiah. He was a member of a family of priests who lived in Anathoth, a town just north of the city of Jerusalem.

The Lord first spoke to Jeremiah in the thirteenth year of the reign of Josiah. He said,

> Before I formed you inside your mother,
>   I chose you;
> before you were born,
>   I set you apart
>   and appointed you
>   to be prophet to the nations.

"O my Lord God!" answered Jeremiah. "Look—I don't know how to speak! I'm just a boy!"

"Never say you're just a boy!" said the Lord. "But go where I send you, and say what I tell you. Don't be afraid, for I am with you, and I'll rescue you from your enemies."

Then the Lord stretched out his hand and touched Jeremiah's mouth and said,

> There! I've put my words into your mouth!
> See! I've given you authority today
> over nations and kingdoms
> to uproot and to tear down,
> to ruin and to destroy,
> to build and to plant.

> Go! Shout into the ears of Jerusalem!
> Tell the people what I have said!

Jeremiah went out into the streets of the city and preached to the people. "Hear the word of the Lord!" he cried. "The Lord remembers how you used to love him, as a young bride loves her husband. Once you were faithful, but now you have left the Lord to run after other gods. You have rebelled against the Lord your God, so he says to you,

> My people have left me,
> the fountain of living water,
> to dig wells for themselves,
> leaky cisterns
> that can't hold water!"

Jeremiah hoped that Josiah's reforms would encourage the people to turn to the Lord. He thought they would humble themselves and change their behavior. But he was disappointed, for most people changed only on the outside. Although they destroyed the pagan altars and promised to obey the Lord, inside they were just the same as ever.

Then the Lord sent Jeremiah a vision.

"What do you see?" he asked.

"A bubbling pot," answered Jeremiah. "As it boils, it tips over from the north side."

"Disaster is coming from the north!" said the Lord. "It will strike all the people who live in the land. I'm calling the kings of the north to come and set up their thrones right in front of the gates of Jerusalem! I'm going to punish the people for leaving me and worshiping idols, for all their crimes and wicked behavior!

"As for you, Jeremiah, be prepared! Stand up and prophesy to the people as I tell you. Don't be afraid of them, for I've made you as strong as a fortress. They'll attack you, but they can never defeat you, for I am with you, and I'll rescue you from your enemies."

Jeremiah traveled all over the land to warn the people of the disaster that was coming. He told them what the Lord had shown to him.

Then the Lord said, "Go through the streets of Jerusalem. Search everywhere for someone who obeys my commandments. If you find just one person who does justice, then I'll pardon the whole city!"

Jeremiah went back and forth through Jerusalem, looking for just one person who obeyed the Lord. But he found only liars, cheats, and thieves.

"Well," he said to himself. "I've just seen the common people. They're ignorant. They don't know what the Lord requires. I'll go and see the great men, the wealthy and educated people. Surely, they follow the ways of the Lord!"

But the great men were even worse than the common people.

"Don't speak to us about the Lord!" they said. "We don't believe your visions of disaster. You prophets are all a bunch of windbags. Nothing bad will happen to us!"

"Stupid people!" cried Jeremiah. "You don't believe me, but the Lord is going to punish you. You're fat and rich from lying and stealing. You don't care about the Lord or the poor people around you. Why are you so stubborn? You have eyes, but you don't see. You have ears, but you don't hear. Don't you understand the power of the Lord?"

One day the Lord said to Jeremiah, "Don't marry and have children in this place, for terrible things are going to happen to the families who live here. Don't enter a house where they're having a funeral. Don't give sympathy to mourners. For the time is coming when people will die in this place without funerals, without sympathy, without mourners. And don't enter a house where they're celebrating a wedding. Don't sit with them, eating and drinking. For I'm going to take away all their joy. They'll be without brides, without grooms, without wedding feasts.

"Go, tell the people why you won't marry or attend funerals and weddings. Explain that I'm going to throw them out of this land and into a foreign land where they can serve all the gods they want. I won't have pity on them anymore!"

Jeremiah did as the Lord commanded. He didn't marry and have children. He didn't attend weddings and funerals. His whole life was a sign to show the people what the Lord was going to do, a sign of the great disaster that was coming to Jerusalem and Judah.

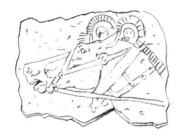

20

The Fall of Nineveh

2 Kings 23; 2 Chronicles 35; Nahum

EARLY in the reign of King Josiah, Assyria became weak. As the empire collapsed, other nations took over Assyrian territory. Josiah himself claimed power over the land of Israel.

Then the Lord gave a vision to a man named Nahum. Nahum saw the destruction of Nineveh, the capital city of the Assyrian Empire.

Nahum went out and told the people of Judah what he had seen. He told them that the Lord was going to punish the Assyrians and destroy Nineveh.

This was good news for Judah and everyone who had suffered from the cruelty of the Assyrians.

"The Lord has humbled his people," said Nahum, "but he'll punish their enemies. The Lord is slow to anger, but his power is enormous. He never lets sin go unpunished. He pours out his fury like fire, completely destroying those who work against him.

"Look!" he cried. "I see a vision of a messenger, hurrying across the mountains. He's bringing good news. Judah's enemy has been destroyed. It's time to celebrate.

"A great new power is rising against the Assyrians. An enormous army will come to attack Nineveh and carry away all its treasures. The city will become an empty wasteland. The people of Nineveh will be so frightened, their knees will give way and their faces will become pale.

"The Lord will punish Nineveh as Nineveh has oppressed the nations. For Nineveh is a city soaked in blood, full of lies, and stuffed with loot! Everyone who hears the news of the fall of Nineveh will clap their hands!"

A few years later Nahum's prophecy came true. The armies of the Medes and the Chaldeans entered the city of Nineveh and destroyed it. They pushed the Assyrians westward, to the city of Haran. The Assyrians held out in Haran a few years longer, but their power was broken. Their time of glory was past.

Then Necho, king of Egypt, marched out to help the Assyrians. He was afraid the Chaldeans would attack Egypt if the Assyrians were completely destroyed.

Josiah, king of Judah, sent a message to Necho, telling him to stay home. Josiah was more afraid of the Assyrians than the Chaldeans, and he didn't want the Egyptians to help them.

When Necho received Josiah's message, he answered, "This war I'm fighting is none of your business, king of Judah! I'm not going to attack you. God has told me to hurry, so don't interfere, or he may destroy you."

Although God was speaking to Josiah through

Necho, Josiah went into battle against the Egyptians and the Assyrians. He led his army north and met the Egyptian army at a place called Megiddo. Although he went out in disguise, he was struck by an Egyptian arrow.

"Take me away!" cried Josiah to his servants. "I'm badly wounded!"

Josiah's servants lifted him from his chariot and took him back to Jerusalem, where he died.

The people of Judah mourned a long time for Josiah. Jeremiah the prophet wrote a song about the death of the good, beloved king. Huldah's prophecy was coming true.

21

What Jeremiah Said About the Temple

2 Kings 23; 2 Chronicles 36; Jeremiah 7, 22, 26

DON'T weep for the dead," said Jeremiah to the people of Judah. "Don't mourn for Josiah. Weep instead for Jehoahaz, who will never return to his native land. He'll die a prisoner in a foreign country."

The people had anointed Josiah's son Jehoahaz as king, but then Pharaoh Necho of Egypt had taken Jehoahaz prisoner.

Jeremiah's prophecy came true. Jehoahaz never returned to Judah, but died a prisoner in Egypt. Necho put Jehoahaz's brother Jehoiakim

105

on the throne of Judah and forced him to pay a large amount of gold and silver as tribute to Egypt.

Jehoiakim was unlike his father. Josiah was honest and fair and treated the people with justice. But Jehoiakim was a wicked king, like his grandfather, Amon. He encouraged the people to worship idols, and he built pagan altars all over the land. He forced the poor to work for him without pay, to build him a great new palace, panel its large rooms with cedar wood, and paint it bright red.

Jeremiah warned Jehoiakim that God would punish him if he didn't change his behavior. But Jehoiakim ignored Jeremiah. He was interested only in himself, not in doing justice and obeying the Lord.

One day the Lord said to Jeremiah, "Go, stand in the courtyard of the temple and speak to the people as they come to worship. Perhaps this time they'll pay attention. If they turn from their evil ways, I won't bring disaster to them."

Jeremiah went up to the temple and spoke to the people. "Hear the word of the Lord!" he cried. "If you turn from your wicked ways, the Lord will be with you. But don't think he's with you in this temple when you disobey him. Don't think you're safe from disaster because God's temple is in Jerusalem.

"You believe you don't have to obey his commandments. You believe he'll never let your enemies defeat you. Well, you're trusting in a lie! You think you can do anything—lie, steal, murder, commit adultery, worship idols—and then come in here and pray and be safe. You're like a gang of thieves, hiding in your den after you commit your robberies!

"Remember what happened to the holy place at Shiloh. The Lord let the Philistines come and destroy it. If you don't listen to the Lord, he'll treat this temple just as he treated the tabernacle at Shiloh.

"And remember what happened to the Northern Kingdom. If you don't pay attention to the Lord, he'll drive you out, just as he drove out the people of Samaria."

When the priests and the prophets and the people heard Jeremiah say that the temple would be destroyed, they were shocked. They thought the Lord would never let them be defeated; they believed he would be with them no matter how they behaved. And now that Nineveh was destroyed, they weren't afraid of the Assyrians.

"You'll die for saying these things!" cried the priests and prophets, and they seized Jeremiah. "Why have you prophesied in the Lord's name? Why do you say this temple will be destroyed and this city will become a wasteland?"

The people crowded around Jeremiah, and someone went down to the palace and told the nobles what was going on. The nobles came up and took their seats by the gate, where they judged cases. Then the priests and the prophets spoke against Jeremiah.

"This man deserves to die," they said. "He has spoken against Jerusalem! You heard him with your own ears."

Jeremiah said, "The Lord himself sent me. He told me to prophesy. If you pay attention to the Lord and change your behavior—if you do justice to one another and stop worshiping foreign gods—then the Lord will show mercy to you! You'll escape the disaster he's preparing to send to this temple and this city.

"As for me, I'm in your power. Do whatever you think is right. But if you put me to death, you'll be guilty of spilling innocent blood. For the

Lord himself has sent me to say these things to you!"

The nobles and the people said to the priests and prophets, "This man doesn't deserve to die! He has spoken to us in the name of the Lord our God."

Then some of the nobles stood up and spoke to the crowd. "There was a prophet named Micah from Moresheth," they said. "Micah prophesied when Hezekiah was king. He said Zion would become a plowed field, Jerusalem would become a pile of ruins, and the mountain of the temple would return to woodland. But Hezekiah and the people didn't kill him. They listened to Micah, and the Lord showed mercy to them. The Lord defended Jerusalem from Sennacherib and the Assyrians. If we kill Jeremiah, the Lord will punish us!"

Then Ahikam, the son of Shaphan the scribe, saved Jeremiah's life. He protected him from the priests and prophets and kept them from handing Jeremiah over to the people to be put to death.

Jeremiah was in real danger, for King Jehoiakim had already executed a prophet named Uriah for saying the same things about Jerusalem and the temple.

22

The Suffering Prophet

*2 Kings 24; 2 Chronicles 36; Jeremiah 8—12,
14—15, 20, 25, 46—49*

EARLY in the reign of Jehoiakim, the Assyrian Empire disappeared. It was replaced in the northeast by the Medes and in the southwest by the Chaldeans . The Chaldeans of Babylon fought against the Egyptians for control of the territory that included Judah.

The Chaldean king Nabopolasser stayed in Babylon while his son Prince Nebuchadnezzar marched out to claim their new empire. Nebuchadnezzar met and defeated Pharaoh Necho's army at Carchemish, an Egyptian military base on the Euphrates River near the place where King Josiah had been killed four years earlier. Then Nabopolasser died, and Nebuchadnezzar returned to Babylon to become king.

Jehoiakim was still under the power of the Egyptians, but after the battle of Carchemish he realized that he would soon have to pay tribute to the Chaldeans.

At about the same time Jeremiah realized that the Lord was going to use Nebuchadnezzar as his instrument to punish Judah and the other nations. The Lord sent visions to Jeremiah, showing him the great disaster that was coming.

"Take this cup of wine from my hand," said the Lord. "Give it to all the nations and make them drink from it, so they'll stumble and fall down."

In his vision Jeremiah offered the cup to the Egyptians, the Philistines, the Edomites, the Moabites, the Ammonites, the Phoenicians, and all the other nations.

"Tell them they must drink from the cup," said the Lord. "For I'm going to send disaster to them. No one will escape!"

Then Jeremiah saw a vision of the suffering of Judah and Jerusalem as enemies from the north came and invaded the land. Jeremiah loved his people so much, it hurt him to see such things and have to tell about them.

"I can't stand it!" he cried. "My heart is sick at the sight of so much misery. Oh, I wish my head were water and my eyes a fountain of tears, so I

111

could cry all day and all night for my people."

Jeremiah went out and warned the people, saying, "I've been speaking to you for twenty-three years. I've told you to turn from your idols, to change your way of living, so the Lord will let you stay in the land. But you won't listen to me. You won't listen to any of the prophets the Lord sends. So now the Lord is going to send for Nebuchadnezzar, king of Babylon. He'll come with the Chaldean army and attack this nation and all the other nations, too. The whole land will become a wasteland, and the people of Judah will be taken into captivity for seventy years. They'll stay in exile until the Lord breaks the power of Babylon!"

Then the Lord said to Jeremiah, "Keep on speaking to the people, even though they ignore you. Go into all the towns of Judah and into the streets of Jerusalem and tell them what I say."

"Yes, Lord," answered Jeremiah, and he went out and spoke to the people.

"Hear the word of the Lord," Jeremiah cried. "Obey his commandments, and he'll be with you. Remember the covenant he made with you and your ancestors. If you get rid of your idols and obey the Lord, he'll be your God. He'll rescue you from your enemies."

But everywhere Jeremiah went, the people refused to listen. Even in his hometown of Anathoth, they hated his message.

Jeremiah didn't realize how angry the people

were until the Lord said, "Your own brothers are against you. They criticize you behind your back. Don't believe them when they act friendly."

Then the men of Anathoth came to Jeremiah and said, "Don't prophesy in the name of the Lord, or we'll kill you."

"Help me, Lord!" cried Jeremiah. "Punish these people."

"Stop complaining," the Lord answered. "If you're tired and discouraged while you're running a simple footrace, how will you be able to run against horses? You're suffering now, but things will become worse."

The Lord's words came true. As Jeremiah preached in the towns of Judah and the streets of Jerusalem, the people began to plot against him.

"Everybody laughs at me!" complained Jeremiah. "When I speak, they criticize me. I'm sorry I was ever born. I've done nothing wrong, but everyone hates me. I sit alone while they laugh and have a good time. I'm just trying to serve you, Lord. Please help me."

"Stop whining!" said the Lord. "If you stop complaining, I'll let you keep on serving me. Don't be afraid. I'll protect you from your enemies. They won't defeat you, for I'll rescue you from their power."

"O, Lord," said Jeremiah, "You have overpowered me. I can hear voices in the crowd plotting against me—even the people who used to be my friends. But you're at my side, Lord, fighting for me. Praise the Lord, for he'll save me from the power of my enemies!"

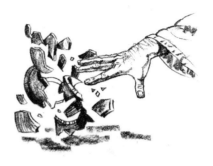

23

Jeremiah Smashes a Pot

Jeremiah 18—20

ONE day the Lord said to Jeremiah, "Go down to the potter's house right now. I'll tell you what to say when you get there."

Jeremiah went down to the potter's house, and there he found the potter busy working at his wheel. Sometimes the pot he was making came out wrong, and then the potter reshaped the clay into something new.

As Jeremiah watched the potter at work, the Lord said to him, "Tell the people they're responsible for bringing punishment on themselves. I treat them as this potter treats his clay. When I make something and it doesn't turn out right, I destroy it. If they continue to disobey me, I'll destroy them; if they turn from their wicked ways, I'll bless them."

Jeremiah told the people about his visit to the potter's house. He warned them that the Lord would destroy them if they continued with their wrong behavior.

Another day the Lord said to Jeremiah, "Go, buy a clay pot. Then go with the leaders and the priests to a place outside the city. Smash the pot near the pagan altar outside the city gate. While you're there, give my message to the people."

Jeremiah went and bought a clay pot from a potter. Then he went with the leaders and priests

to the valley of Hinnon, the terrible place where King Manasseh had offered his sons to idols. There he smashed the pot.

"See what I've done!" cried Jeremiah. "The Lord will break this people and this city as I have broken this pot! And nobody will be able to put you back together again. This pagan altar where you offer sacrifices to idols will become a graveyard. The whole city will become a graveyard, for the people of Jerusalem will be slaughtered by their enemies."

Then Jeremiah returned to the city. He went and stood in the courtyard of the temple and spoke to the people.

A priest named Pashhur, who was in charge of the temple, ordered the guards to beat Jeremiah and put him in the stocks near the gate. They locked Jeremiah's feet in a long block of wood and left him there overnight.

The next morning Pashhur came and let Jeremiah out of the stocks.

Then Jeremiah said, "The Lord's name for you isn't Pashhur, but Terror! He's going to hand you over to terror, and your enemies will kill you. The Lord will hand all of Judah over to the king of Babylon, and he'll carry them into captivity. You and your family will be taken to Babylon, and you'll die there, for you've been prophesying lies to the people!"

After this Jeremiah was set free, but he wasn't allowed to go into the temple anymore.

24

The King Burns Jeremiah's Scroll

Jeremiah 36, 45

THAT same year the Lord said to Jeremiah, "Go and buy a book-sized scroll and write down everything I've told you. Write everything I've said since the day I first sent you to be a prophet. If the people hear about the disaster I'm planning to send, perhaps they'll turn from their wicked ways, and I can forgive them."

Jeremiah asked his friend Baruch to help him. As Jeremiah dictated the words the Lord had said to him, Baruch acted as a scribe and wrote everything down on the scroll in ink.

In the winter of the next year the Chaldean army attacked the Philistine city of Ashekelon, near Judah, and destroyed it. In this dangerous situation, the people of Judah went to the temple for a day of prayer and fasting.

Jeremiah decided it would be a good time for the people to hear the word of the Lord as it was written on the scroll. So he said to Baruch, "I'm not allowed to enter the temple. You go for me and read the scroll to the people of Judah and Jerusalem. Perhaps they'll pay attention this time and turn from their sins, for the Lord is very angry with them."

Baruch went up to the temple and read the scroll to the people. He stood in the upper courtyard, in a place where everyone could see and hear him.

Micaiah, the grandson of Shaphan the royal scribe, heard what Baruch was saying, and he went immediately to the palace, to the room where the nobles were meeting. He reported what he had heard to his father, Gemariah, and the other nobles.

They decided to send a man named Jehudi to the temple to bring Baruch to the palace. Jehudi went to Baruch and said, "Come with me, and bring the scroll with you."

As soon as Baruch arrived at the palace, the nobles said, "Please sit down and read the scroll to us."

Baruch read them the warnings, the visions,

and the promises that the Lord had given to Jeremiah.

The nobles listened carefully. Then they turned to each other in alarm, saying, "We'll certainly have to report this to the king!

"Now tell us," they said to Baruch, "how did you happen to write these things?"

"Jeremiah dictated them to me," answered Baruch. "I just wrote down what he said."

"Go and hide!" they warned. "You and Jeremiah are in great danger. Don't let anyone know where you are."

Baruch left the palace, and the nobles took the scroll and put it in the room of Elishama, the royal scribe. Then they went in to see the king.

When King Jehoiakim heard what was going

on, he sent Jehudi to bring the scroll and read it to him aloud.

"I don't believe these things!" said Jehoiakim. "I don't believe that the king of Babylon is coming to destroy this land."

He and his advisers weren't alarmed like the nobles. They didn't cry in sorrow for their sins. Instead of being afraid of the Lord, they were angry with Jeremiah.

It was wintertime, and Jehoiakim was sitting in his winter apartment, with a fire burning in a small stove in front of him. As Jehudi unrolled the scroll and read three or four columns of writing, Jehoiakim cut the scroll with a scribe's penknife and tossed the pieces into the fire. He did this until the entire scroll was burned up.

Gemariah and the other nobles begged Jehoiakim not to destroy the scroll, but he paid no attention to them. He ordered his officials to arrest Baruch and Jeremiah. But when they went out to look for them, they couldn't find them, for the Lord had hidden them.

Then the Lord said to Jeremiah, "Go and get another scroll and write down everything that was on the first one. Tell Jehoiakim that I'm going to punish him because he dared to burn the scroll and because he didn't believe what was written on it. Jehoiakim will have no sons to rule after him. When he dies, his body will be tossed away without a decent burial. I'll punish him and his family, his officials, and the people of

Jerusalem and Judah, for they have refused to listen to me!"

Then Jeremiah took another scroll and gave it to Baruch. Baruch wrote down everything Jeremiah said. He wrote down all the words that were on the first scroll and many new ones, too.

As he was writing, Baruch sighed. "Poor me! I have problems enough, and now the Lord is bringing this great disaster!" he exclaimed.

Jeremiah answered, The Lord is going to strike the whole earth, Baruch, and here you are asking for special treatment! Don't ask, for God's going to bring disaster to everyone. As for you, hear what the Lord says about you—he'll let you escape with your life, wherever you may go!"

25

A Good Example

2 Kings 24; 2 Chronicles 36; Jeremiah 35

JEHOIAKIM switched his loyalty from the Egyptians to the Chaldeans. He paid tribute to Nebuchadnezzar, king of Babylon, for three years. Then the Egyptians showed strength against the Chaldeans, and Jehoiakim changed sides again.

Nebuchadnezzar sent some troops to Judah to put down the rebellion. He didn't send his whole army, but some imperial soldiers, for the rebellion in Judah seemed to be just one more small, local problem. The country people were so

123

afraid of the Chaldean raiders, they came into the city of Jerusalem for safety.

Then the Lord said to Jeremiah, "Go and find the members of the Rechabite community. Speak with them and bring them to one of the private rooms of the temple and offer them some wine to drink."

The Rechabites were the descendants of Jonadab, son of Rechab. For two hundred and fifty years they had been living in the wilderness, following the strict rules of their ancestor.

Jeremiah found the leaders of the community and brought them to the temple, to the room of Ben-Hanan, a temple prophet. He put pitchers of wine and some cups in front of them and said, "Have some wine!"

"We don't drink wine," answered the Rechabites. "Our ancestor, Jonadab, told us not to. He also told us not to build houses or plant crops or buy property. We live in tents. We faithfully obey all of Jonadab's commandments. We came into the city only because of the Chaldeans."

Jeremiah said to the Rechabites, "The Lord is pleased with you for faithfully obeying your ancestor's commandments. He will reward you by seeing that Jonadab's family will not die out; Jonadab will always have descendants to serve the Lord God of Israel!"

Then Jeremiah went out and told the people of Jerusalem and Judah about the Rechabites.

"Hear the word of the Lord!" he said. "The

Rechabites are a good example for the people of Jerusalem and Judah. Learn a lesson in faithfulness from them. They've completely obeyed their ancestor. Even today they don't drink wine. The Lord has spoken to you over and over, but you pay no attention to him. He has sent prophets to warn you, but you won't listen. The Rechabites obey their ancestor, but you disobey God. He will punish you by sending a great disaster to Jerusalem and Judah!"

26

Habakkuk's Complaint

Habakkuk

A prophet of Judah named Habakkuk was upset with the Lord when he saw the terrible suffering that the Chaldeans were causing.

"Lord," he asked, "how long must I cry out for help without an answer from you? I see violence all around me. Everywhere I look, wicked people are winning against righteous people. It isn't fair. Why do you let it happen?"

"Look at the nations," answered the Lord. "You'll be amazed at what I'm doing. I'm stirring up those fierce and fiery Chaldeans to march across the nations, invading and conquering. They ride on horseback, swifter than leopards. They fight more fiercely than wolves in the dark. They gallop in suddenly, swooping up prisoners like sand."

"O Lord, my God!" cried Habakkuk. "You are the power behind the Chaldeans. You're the one who has made them your instrument for punishing the nations! But why do you let them treat us so cruelly? Why don't you do something when evil people destroy those who are better than they? Look at them: they catch everyone in their net. They slaughter whole nations without pity!"

Habakkuk watched and waited to see what the Lord would say. What answer would he give to his complaints?

Finally, the Lord said, "I'm sending you a vision. Write it on tablets, large enough for everyone to see. Some day this vision will come true. If it seems slow in coming, wait for it, for it will certainly happen. The wicked will fail. But for now, the righteous will live by being faithful."

Habakkuk saw a vision of the Lord coming in power to save his people and to punish evil. Then he said to the people,

The Lord is in his holy temple;
let all the earth keep silence before him.

Then Habakkuk said,

Even if the trees produce no fruit,
　　and all the crops fail
　　　　and all the sheep and cattle die,

Still I will rejoice in the Lord;
　　I will be happy because of God, my savior!
　　　　The Lord is my strength;
　　　　　　he makes my feet like a deer's,
　　　　　　　　and he watches over me on the high places.

The Last Days of
Judah

27

The Rotten Figs

2 Kings 24—25; 2 Chronicles 36; Jeremiah 13, 22—24

NEBUCHADNEZZAR was marching toward Judah with his army to crush Jehoiakim's rebellion. Before he arrived, Jehoiakim died and his son Jehoiachin became king.

Then Jeremiah the prophet said, "Tell Jehoiachin to come down from his throne, for his glorious crown is going to fall off his head! The people of Judah are going to be carried into exile!"

That spring Jeremiah's words came true. Nebuchadnezzar attacked Judah. After a three-month siege, Jehoiachin surrendered. The help promised by the Egyptians never arrived, and Judah was no match for the Chaldeans. Nebuchadnezzar took Jehoiachin prisoner and carried him into exile in Babylon. He also carried away the gold equipment of the temple and the treasures of Jehoiachin's palace. He took a total of seven thousand people to Babylon: nobles, royal officials, skilled workers, and blacksmiths, as well as the king and his five sons.

Then Jeremiah said, "Jehoiachin wouldn't listen to the Lord when all was well. Ever since he was a young man, he refused to listen to the Lord. Now he and his officials are going into exile. Like his uncle Jehoahaz, who was taken prisoner to Egypt, Jehoiachin will never return. He'll die in a foreign land, and none of his children will ever rule Judah."

Jeremiah added words of hope to this message. "Someday," he said, "the Lord will gather the remnant of his flock. They've been scattered like sheep by bad shepherds. The Lord will raise up good shepherds and bring them back to the land. A descendant of David will rule over them, and in that day the Lord will save his people."

Jeremiah's prophecy began to come true. Jehoiachin stayed in Babylon for the rest of his life. He never returned to the land of Judah, and none of his sons became king.

Nebuchadnezzar put Mattaniah, on the throne of Judah. He was another one of Josiah's sons and a brother of Jehoiakim and Jehoahaz. Nebuchadnezzar renamed the new king Zedekiah. King Zedekiah took an oath, promising to be loyal to King Nebuchadnezzar of Babylon.

After Jehoiachin was taken away and his uncle Zedekiah became king, the Lord showed Jeremiah a vision. Jeremiah was standing in front of the temple when he noticed two baskets of figs. In one basket were excellent, early-ripening fruit. The other basket contained rotten figs.

"What do you see, Jeremiah?" asked the Lord.

"Figs," he answered. "The good ones are ex-

cellent, but the bad ones are so rotten, they're inedible."

Then the Lord said, "The exiles I've sent to Babylon are like these good figs. I'll watch over them and bring them back to this land. I'll show them that I am the Lord, and they'll turn to me with their whole hearts. They'll be my people, and I'll be their God.

"But the ones who have been left behind are like the rotten figs. They'll become a laughingstock and a curse, an object of shame for the whole world to see. I'll send war, starvation, and disease to them until they disappear from this land!"

28

Jeremiah Wears a Yoke

Jeremiah 27—29, 51

FOUR years after Jehoiakim's rebellion against Nebuchadnezzar, the leaders of Judah began to plot again. Pharaoh Hophra, king of Egypt, was encouraging all the kings in the western part of the Chaldean Empire to rebel.

Zedekiah was a weak king. He followed the advice of his officials and agreed to join the new rebellion.

Ambassadors from the kings of Edom, Moab, Ammon, Tyre, and Sidon came to Jerusalem to meet with Zedekiah. They came to his palace to talk about their plans to rebel against Nebuchadnezzar.

Then the Lord said to Jeremiah, "Make some leather cords and a wooden yoke bar. Tie the yoke across the back of your neck, like the yoke a farmer puts on the neck of an ox. Then go see the foreign ambassadors and show them the yoke and speak to them as I tell you."

Jeremiah made the cords and the yoke and tied the yoke to his shoulders. He went to the palace to show this sign of slavery to the ambassadors.

"See!" he said to them. "The Lord God, Creator of the whole earth, has handed all the nations over to Nebuchadnezzar, king of Babylon. Your nations will be his subjects, and the subjects of his son and grandson, until the time has come for the Lord to destroy Babylon. Everyone who refuses to bow down and put his neck under the yoke of Nebuchadnezzar will be punished!"

Jeremiah told the ambassadors to go back to their kings and tell them it was God's will for Nebuchadnezzar's yoke to be put on their necks. They must submit to the power of Babylon or be destroyed.

Then Jeremiah turned to the king and nobles of Judah and said, "Bend your necks to the yoke of the king of Babylon! If you submit to Nebuchadnezzar, you'll live. The Lord will let you stay in this land. But if you listen to the prophets who tell you not to give in, you'll go into exile. Those prophets are lying. The Lord hasn't sent them. If you do as they say, you'll die!"

Jeremiah left the palace and went up to the temple to speak to the priests and the people. He kept the yoke on his neck as a sign.

"Hear the word of the Lord," said Jeremiah. "He says not to listen to the people who tell you everything will be all right. The false prophets are saying that the temple equipment will soon be brought back from Babylon. They're wrong! The Lord is going to let the Chaldeans come to Jerusalem and take everything that's left in the temple!"

That same year a prophet named Hananiah was speaking to the priests and the people at the temple. His message was just the opposite of Jeremiah's.

"Hear the word of the Lord!" cried Hananiah. "The Lord has broken the yoke of the king of Babylon! Two years from now he'll bring back all the temple equipment that was taken away. He'll bring back Jehoiachin and the others who were carried into exile!"

"Amen!" said Jeremiah. "I hope you're right. May the Lord do as you say. May he bring back the exiles and the temple equipment. But listen to me. From the earliest times all the Lord's prophets have prophesied war, starvation, and disease. Those who prophesy peace are true prophets only if their words come true."

Then Hananiah snatched the yoke from Jeremiah's neck and broke it, saying, "This is how the Lord will break the yoke of the king of Babylon and take it off the necks of the nations."

Jeremiah left quietly, saying no more.

A little while later the Lord sent Jeremiah to Hananiah with a message. "All right," said Jeremiah. "You've broken the wooden yoke. But now the Lord will make iron yokes and place them on the necks of all the nations.

"Listen, Hananiah! The Lord hasn't sent you. You've been encouraging the people to trust in a lie. Therefore, the Lord says he'll really send you—right off the face of the earth! This very year you'll die, for you've told lies in the name of the Lord!"

Two months later Jeremiah's words came true, and Hananiah died.

The next year Jeremiah wrote a letter to the Judean exiles in Babylon. He sent the letter with Elasah and Gemariah, who were taking a message from Zedekiah to Nebuchadnezzar.

Jeremiah's letter said:

"The Lord of power and might, the God of Israel, tells all the exiles he has sent to Babylon: Build houses and settle down. Plant gardens and eat what they produce. Marry and have children. Choose wives for your sons and husbands for your daughters. Encourage them to raise families. Work for the good of the land you're living in. Pray to the Lord for its good, for your good depends on its good.

"Beware of false prophets who say you'll soon

return to Judah. The Lord says he'll bring you back after seventy years have passed. He plans a great future for you, full of peace and hope. When you pray to him, he'll hear you. When you seek him with your whole heart, he'll let you find him."

That same year Zedekiah went to Babylon to bow down before Nebuchadnezzar. Among the officials who went with him was Seraiah, the brother of Jeremiah's friend Baruch.

Jeremiah gave Seraiah a message written on a piece of paper. It was a prophecy of all the evil that would happen to Babylon in the future.

Jeremiah said to Seraiah, "When you arrive in Babylon, be sure to read all these words aloud.

Then say, 'O Lord, you yourself have said that you'll destroy this place and make it a wasteland!' After you finish reading the message, tie a stone to the paper and throw it into the Euphrates River. Say, 'Just as this paper is sinking, so will Babylon sink and never rise again! For someday the Lord will send a great disaster and destroy Babylon!'

"The day is coming when the Lord will punish the idols of Babylon. The whole country will be put to shame. The city will be burned down; its greatness will be destroyed. This is how the work of the nations comes to nothing; the power of Babylon will end in fire."

29

A Broken Promise

Jeremiah 21, 34

KING Zedekiah of Judah was a weak and frightened man. His advisers and the Egyptians were pressuring him to rebel against the Chaldeans.

Finally they convinced him that Judah could break free, that the power of Egypt would save him.

So Zedekiah refused to send tribute to Nebuchadnezzar, and Nebuchadnezzar sent an army to Judah. For several months the Chaldeans attacked the fortresses outside Jerusalem, pushing

Zedekiah's soldiers back toward the city.

This frightened Zedekiah so much, he sent some of his officials to Jeremiah, to ask for his help.

"Please consult the Lord for us," they said. "The king of Babylon is attacking us. Perhaps the Lord might work a miracle and force the Chaldeans to leave Judah."

They were remembering how the Lord had defended Jerusalem from Sennacherib and the Assyrians when Hezekiah was king, a hundred years earlier.

But Jeremiah answered, "Tell Zedekiah that the Lord is going to let your army be defeated. He's going to pull the Chaldeans right into this city. The Lord himself will fight against you, with lashing fist and mighty arm! He'll strike down the people of Jerusalem and hand the survivors over to the Chaldeans.

"Tell the people of Jerusalem that the Lord will let them choose between life and death. If they stay in the city, they'll die. But if they surrender to the Chaldeans now, they'll live. The Lord is so angry with Jerusalem, he's going to hand it over to Nebuchadnezzar and let him burn it to the ground!"

Zedekiah's officials took this message to the king, but the king and his advisers paid no attention. Instead of trusting in the Lord, they trusted in the Egyptians to rescue them.

Then suddenly the Chaldeans broke off their

attack. They heard that the Egyptians were marching out to meet them, so Nebuchadnezzar pulled his army out of Judah and went out to fight the Egyptians.

When this happened, Zedekiah sent his officials to Jeremiah again, and Jeremiah said, "Tell the king that the Lord is going to bring the Chaldeans back to Judah. They'll attack and capture Jerusalem and burn it to the ground! The Lord will make this place a wasteland, and he'll hand Zedekiah and his officials over to Nebuchadnezzar's army.

"The Egyptians aren't going to defeat the Chaldeans. They're going to turn around and go home. Nothing can stop the Chaldeans from destroying Jerusalem. Even if you struck them

all down and only the wounded were left, the Lord would raise them up from their beds and bring them back!"

But Zedekiah and his advisers continue to ignore Jeremiah's advice. While the Chaldeans were gone, life returned to normal.

When the Chaldeans were attacking Jerusalem, King Zedekiah and the people of the city made a promise in the name of the Lord. They agreed to set free all their Hebrew slaves. But as soon as the Chaldeans left, and they thought the danger was over, they took back their slaves.

This made the Lord even more angry with the people of Jerusalem.

"I made a covenant with these people when I freed them from slavery in Egypt," he said to Jeremiah. "They know they shouldn't keep their fellow Hebrews as slaves. They have broken their promise, and they must be punished!"

30

Jeremiah in the Pit

Jeremiah 37—39

At this time Jeremiah decided to go to Anathoth to take care of some family business. As he was going out the gate of Jerusalem, an officer of the guard named Irijah seized him.

"You're deserting to the Chaldeans!" cried Irijah.

"That's a lie!" answered Jeremiah. "I'm not deserting."

But Irijah refused to listen. He arrested Jeremiah and took him to the city officials.

The officials were furious with Jeremiah because he had been telling the people to surrender to the Chaldeans. They gave orders for the prophet to be beaten and put into a dungeon.

Then they went to the king and said, "Put this man to death, for he's hurting the city. He's discouraging our soldiers and our people. He doesn't care about Jerusalem. He wants us to be destroyed!"

"Very well," answered Zedekiah. "He's in your hands. I can't stop you."

Jeremiah was taken and thrown into a cistern, a deep pit which was used for storing water. The pit contained no water, but it was full of mud. As Jeremiah was let down with ropes, he sank into the mud.

A palace official named Ebed-Melek, an Ethiopian, heard what was going on. He waited for the king to go out to the city gate to judge cases, and then he went to him and said, "My lord king! The men who have thrown Jeremiah the prophet into the cistern have committed a great crime! They've left him down there to die!"

"All right," answered Zedekiah. "Take three of my servants and go get Jeremiah. Pull him out of the cistern before he dies."

Ebed-Melek went to a room in the palace where clothing was stored and took some odds and ends. He lowered them with ropes to Jeremiah in the pit. "Just put these rags under your arms," said Ebed-Melek. "They'll pad you against the ropes so they don't cut you."

Jeremiah did as he was told. Then Ebed-Melek and Zedekiah's three servants pulled Jeremiah up from the pit with the ropes.

After he escaped from the pit, Jeremiah was kept in the guardhouse. One day while he was there, the king sent for him.

Zedekiah met Jeremiah at the private royal entrance to the temple, where no one could see or hear them.

"I want to ask you something," he said. "Don't keep anything from me."

Jeremiah answered, "If I speak openly, won't you have me put to death? And if I give you good advice, won't you ignore it?"

"I promise," said Zedekiah, "as the Lord lives, who gives us life, I promise I won't have you put to death; I won't hand you over to your enemies!"

"All right," said Jeremiah. "I'll tell you exactly what the Lord has said. If you obey the Lord and surrender to the Chaldeans, he'll let you live, and the city won't be destroyed. You'll die peacefully, with a proper funeral and burial.

"But if you don't surrender, the city will be burned down. You and your family will be handed over as prisoners to Nebuchadnezzar. You'll see him face-to-face, talk with him, and go with him to Babylon!"

"I'm afraid!" cried Zedekiah. "Some Judeans have already deserted to the Chaldeans. What if I'm handed over to them? They'll torture me!"

"Don't worry," said Jeremiah. "That won't

148

happen. Obey the Lord, I beg you! If you listen to his voice, everything will be all right. But if you refuse to obey, terrible things will happen.

"The Lord has shown me a vision of the fall of Jerusalem. I've seen the women of your palace being led away by Nebuchadnezzar's officers. I've seen all your wives and children being brought to the Chaldeans—and you with them!"

Then Zedekiah said, "Don't tell anyone what we've been talking about. If you let anyone know about this secret meeting, you'll die. My officials will find out that I've been speaking to you, and they'll come and ask you what we said. They'll threaten to kill you if you don't tell them. Just say you were asking me not to send you back to prison."

A little while later the king's officials came and questioned Jeremiah. He told them what Zedekiah had ordered him to say. Then they left him alone, for nobody had heard their conversation.

Sometime after this the Lord gave Jeremiah a special message for Ebed-Melek the Ethiopian. Jeremiah said to him, "The Lord will surely bring disaster to this city; you'll see his words come true. But on that day he'll rescue you, for you have put your trust in the Lord."

31

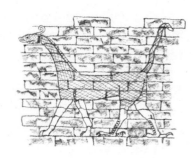

The Fall of Jerusalem

2 Kings 25; 2 Chronicles 36; Jeremiah 32—33, 39

AS Jeremiah had prophesied, the Egyptians went home and the Chaldeans returned to Judah. Nebuchadnezzar's army captured the last two fortresses outside Jerusalem. Then they came with their chariots, horsemen, and foot soldiers, and attacked the city.

During the long months when Jerusalem was being besieged, the Lord said to Jeremiah, "Your cousin Hanamel, the son of your uncle Shallum, is going to come and ask you to buy his field at Anathoth."

Just as the Lord had said, Jeremiah's cousin Hanamel came to see him. "Won't you buy my property at Anathoth?" he asked. "I have to sell a field, and I'd like you to buy it to keep it in the family."

Jeremiah realized that this was a sign from the Lord, so he bought the field for seventeen pieces of silver. He weighed the silver on scales and signed a deed of purchase. He sealed the deed and called in some people to witness it. Then he took the deed and gave it and a copy of it to his friend Baruch. He told Baruch to put both the deed and the copy in a clay pot for safekeeping.

Then Jeremiah explained to Baruch and Hanamel and the others that this purchase of a field was a sign from the Lord. "The Lord says houses and fields and vineyards will be bought in this land once again," he said.

When he was alone again, Jeremiah prayed, "O Lord God, Creator of heaven and earth! See how the siege ramps are already in place to capture the city! The Chaldeans will soon destroy Jerusalem! What you said about the great disaster is coming true—and here you have told me to go and buy a field. I don't understand."

"I am the Lord, the God of all people," answered the Lord. "Is anything impossible for me? Someday I'll gather my people and bring them back from exile. In that day they'll buy fields and draw up deeds and witness them. They will be my people, and I will be their God."

Later the Lord said to Jeremiah, "I'll tell you great mysteries. This city is going to be destroyed, for I'm punishing the people for their wickedness. But I'll heal them. I'll build them up again and forgive their sins. Someday the wilderness of Judah and the empty streets of Jerusalem will be filled with shouts of joy, for I'll restore my people to the land.

"And I'll send a king from the family of David to rule with justice and righteousness. He'll save the people, and I'll never reject them again. I'll have pity on them and raise them up."

The siege of Jerusalem lasted eighteen months. The Egyptians never arrived. Finally the

Chaldeans made a break through the wall. In the middle of the summer Jerusalem fell.

The night it happened Zedekiah left the city with his soldiers. They sneaked out through the palace garden and escaped toward the valley of the Jordan River. The Chaldeans chased after them and caught them in the wilderness near Jericho. Zedekiah's soldiers deserted him, and he was captured by the Chaldeans.

They led Zedekiah north, to Nebuchadnezzar's headquarters. Zedekiah saw Nebuchadnezzar face-to-face, and he watched while his officials were put to death. His sons were executed right before his eyes, and then he was blinded and put in chains and carried prisoner to Babylon.

Judah was no longer an independent nation, not even a vassal state, but a province of the Chaldean Empire. For the first time in four hundred years, no king from the family of David reigned in Jerusalem.

About a month after the fall of the city, Nebuzaradan, the commander of Nebuchadnezzar's guard, arrived in Jerusalem. He took all the valuables from the palace and the temple and the mansions of the city. He smashed the shiny bronze pillars in front of the temple, and he sent the gold and silver temple equipment to Babylon.

Then Nebuzaradan ordered his men to stack brush wood beneath the walls of the temple and the palace and the mansions of the city. They set fire to the wood, and the heat of the fire cracked the stones. Then they pulled down the walls of Jerusalem. The city was a wasteland. The prophecies of Isaiah, Micah, and Jeremiah were coming true.

32

The Murder of Gedaliah

2 Kings 25; 2 Chronicles 36; Jeremiah 39—41

UNLIKE the Assyrians, the Chaldeans didn't settle new people in the lands they conquered. They exiled the leaders and left the common people in the land to plant and harvest the crops. Nebuzaradan sent the rich people of Judah to Babylon as slaves and gave their fields and vineyards to the poor.

Nebuchadnezzar ordered Nebuzaradan to find Jeremiah and treat him well. Nebuzaradan sent his men out to look for the prophet, but they couldn't find him. When the city was destroyed,

Jeremiah had been chained along with the other prisoners. Nebuzaradan's men found him outside Jerusalem, walking with a large group of captives toward Babylon.

Nebuzaradan said to Jeremiah, "The Lord your God said disaster would come to this land, and it has. He did what he said he would do, because his people disobeyed him. Now, look! I'm releasing your hands from the chains. If you'd like, you may come with me to Babylon. I'll look after you. If you don't want to, then don't. You may go wherever you wish."

Nebuzaradan gave Jeremiah some food and a present and sent him on his way. Jeremiah went to Mizpah, eight miles north of Jerusalem, where the Judeans were gathering around Gedaliah. Gedaliah was a Judean whom the Chaldeans had set up as governor of the province of Judah. He was the son of Jeremiah's friend Ahikam.

Some Judean commanders and their soldiers had escaped from the Chaldeans. They were hiding out in the countryside, and when they heard that Gedaliah was governor, they went to him at his headquarters. Among them were two officers named Ishmael and Johanan.

Gedaliah said to them, "Don't be afraid to submit to the Chaldeans. If you stay in Judah and obey Nebuchadnezzar, everything will be all right. I'm responsible for your good. I'll stay here at Mizpah, but you can go home and harvest your crops and settle down."

As the news spread, Judeans who had fled across the border to Moab, Ammon, and Edom came home and settled down.

Then one day Johanan and the other Judean officers came to Gedaliah and said, "Have you heard that Baalis, the king of the Ammonites, is sending Ishmael to assassinate you?"

Gedaliah didn't believe them, so a little while later Johanan went to him secretly and said, "Let me go and kill Ishmael. Nobody will ever find out. Why should he assassinate you? If he murders you, everyone who has gathered around you will be scattered again. Why should Judah suffer more trouble and be destroyed?"

"Don't!" said Gedaliah. "What you say about Ishmael isn't true."

Sometime later, in the fall of the year, Ishmael came to Mizpah with ten men. Gedaliah offered them a meal, and as they were eating together, Ishmael and his men leaped up and struck down Gedaliah and all the people with him, both Judeans and Chaldeans.

Ishmael made prisoners of all the people in Mizpah—men, women, and children—including the prophet Jeremiah. He took them and set out for the land of the Ammonites.

Johanan and the other Judean commanders heard about the murder of Gedaliah and they gathered their soldiers and marched out to attack Ishmael. They caught up with him at Gibeon.

Ishmael's prisoners ran to join Johanan. Then Ishmael and his men slipped away, escaping to Ammonite territory.

Johanan and the other officers were afraid to stay in Judah now, for they thought that the Chaldeans would punish them for the murder of Gedaliah. So they led the people they had rescued away, toward the land of Egypt.

Disobedience and Hope

2 Kings 25; Jeremiah 30—31, 42—44, 50—52

HELP us, Jeremiah!" said Johanan and the other officers and people. "Please ask the Lord your God to save us. We beg you—see how few we are! Ask the Lord to show us where to go and what to do."

"Very well," answered Jeremiah. "I'll pray to the Lord your God, as you ask. I'll tell you whatever he says."

"As the Lord is our witness," they promised, "we'll do exactly as he says. Whether we like it or not, we'll obey the voice of the Lord our God."

159

Ten days later Jeremiah called Johanan and the others to tell them what the Lord had said to him.

"The Lord says to stay in Judah. He doesn't want to punish you anymore. If you stay here, he'll take care of you. Don't be afraid of Nebuchadnezzar, for the Lord is with you to rescue you. He'll cause Nebuchadnezzar to have pity on you and let you return to your homes in peace.

"But if you don't listen to the Lord, if you go to the land of Egypt, you'll perish. The sword you're afraid of will overtake you. The starvation you dread will follow you. Everyone who goes to Egypt will die. The Lord will pour his anger out on you as he did on Jerusalem; you'll never see Judah again!"

When they heard Jeremiah's message, Johanan and the other officers said, "You're lying! The Lord didn't send you to tell us this. No! Baruch must have put you up to it. He wants to get us in trouble so the Chaldeans will put us to death or send us to Babylon."

"No!" answered Jeremiah. "The Lord himself is telling you not to go to Egypt. I warn you, you're making a terrible mistake! When you asked me to pray for you, you promised to do whatever the Lord said. Now that I've told you what he says, you don't want to do it."

But none of the people would obey the Lord. Instead of staying in the land of Judah, Johanan and the other officers led them to Egypt, and they took Jeremiah and Baruch with them.

When they arrived at the city of Tahpanhes in Egypt, the Lord said to Jeremiah, "Go get some large stones and bury them in the clay floor at the entrance of Pharaoh's house, in front of all the Judeans. Tell them that Nebuchadnezzar will come and place his throne right above those stones. He'll strike the land of Egypt with disease, exile, and war. He'll set fire to the temple of the Egyptian gods. He'll pick Egypt clean, like a shepherd picking lice from his cloak!"

Jeremiah did as the Lord said, as a sign for the people of the disaster that would overtake them in Egypt. He said to the people, "You've seen the disaster the Lord brought to Jerusalem and Judah; that place is a wasteland because the people disobeyed the Lord. Now he says you must stop worshiping foreign gods, or he'll punish you as he punished Jerusalem!"

"No!" said the people. "We won't listen to a word you say. We'll go on doing exactly as we please. We'll keep on worshiping foreign gods. When we prayed to the Queen of Heaven in Judah, we had plenty to eat. We lived well; no disaster came to us. It was only when we turned away from the Queen of Heaven that we suffered!"

The Queen of Heaven was Ishtar, an Assyrian goddess. Many of the women worshiped her. Now some of them said to Jeremiah, "When we worship the Queen of Heaven, our husbands know exactly what we're doing!"

"Hear the word of the Lord!" cried Jeremiah. "He punished Judah because you worshiped foreign gods and disobeyed his commandments. Now he's going to hand the king of Egypt over to his enemies, just as he handed over the king of Judah to Nebuchadnezzar. He'll destroy you all!"

In these terrible days after the fall of Jerusalem, Jeremiah trusted in God's promises. The Lord gave Jeremiah messages of hope for the future.

He said, "Write down everything I've told you on a scroll. Someday I'll bring all my people back to the land. They will no longer serve foreigners, but they'll serve their God and a wonderful new

king from the family of David. I'll rescue my people from the power of their enemies. I can't let my people perish. I love them with a love that lasts forever. I'll build them up again; I'll lead them home.

"In that day I'll make a new covenant with my people. They broke the old covenant, a law written on a scroll. But the new covenant will be written on their hearts."

The words of the Lord to Jeremiah began to be fulfilled. Jehoiachin, the king of Judah who was a prisoner in Babylon, was pardoned by Nebuchadnezzar's son, Evil-Merodach. Evil-Merodach treated Jehoiachin kindly and gave him a position of honor above the other kings who were in exile in Babylon. He let Jehoiachin exchange his prison clothes for fine robes and eat at the king's table. Although Jehoiachin never returned to Judah, for the rest of his life the king of Babylon took care of all his needs.

Then Jeremiah's vision of the destruction of Babylon came true. The Medes and the Persians defeated the Chaldeans and the power of Babylon came to an end.

For seventy years the exiles from Judah waited for God to restore them, to lead them back to their own land. Then Cyrus, king of Persia, let the people from Judah return home.

God's words to the prophets came true. The future of God's people was as bright and wonderful as the promises of God.

THE WORLD OF ISAIAH AND JEREMIAH

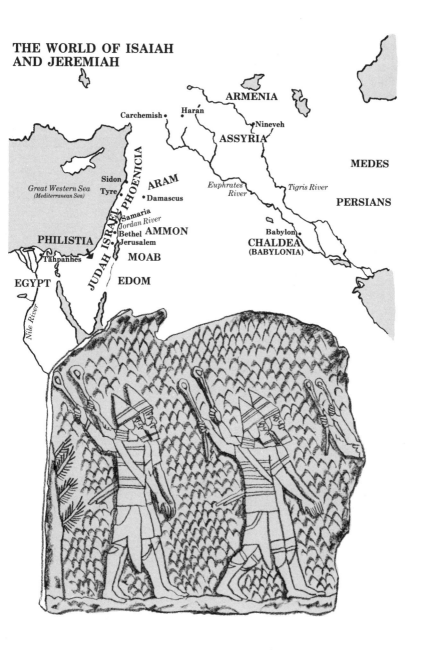

ARMENIA

Carchemish •   • Harán

• Nineveh

ASSYRIA

MEDES

Sidon

Tyre   ARAM

• Damascus

Great Western Sea
(Mediterranean Sea)

Euphrates
River

Tigris River

PERSIANS

PHOENICIA

Samaria
Jordan River

Bethel AMMON

Babylon •

PHILISTIA

Jerusalem

CHALDEA
(BABYLONIA)

Tahpanhes

MOAB

EGYPT   EDOM

JUDAH ISRAEL

Nile River

Eve Bowers MacMaster graduated from the Pennsylvania State University and George Washington University. She also studied at Harvard University and Eastern Mennonite Seminary. She has taught in the Bible department at Eastern Mennonite College and in the history department at James Madison University, both located in Harrisonburg, Virginia.

Eve visited many of the places mentioned in the Bible while she was serving as a Peace Corps Volunteer in Turkey.

Eve and her husband, Richard, live near Harrisonburg, Virginia, with their children, Sam, Tom, and Sarah.